from Grouper to Grits

Delicious Fare with Coastal Flair

JUNIOR LEAGUE OF CLEARWATER-DUNEDIN

From the Chef

Chef John M. Lewis is the Founder, President, and Executive Chef of La Maison Gourmet, Inc. (LMG), in Dunedin, Florida. LMG offers cooking classes to both adults and children in a wide range of cuisine and skill levels, as well as extensive catering services. As the Resident Chef on WFLA-TV's (NBC) Daytime live television show, Chef John Lewis appears every Tuesday to present cooking demonstrations. He has been cooking for thirty-five years and has developed hundreds of recipes. He is also a contributing writer of a monthly column in the IMAGO magazine for the Tampa Bay area.

from Grouper to Grits
Delicious Fare with Coastal Flair

Published by the Junior League of Clearwater-Dunedin, Inc.

The Junior League of Clearwater-Dunedin, Inc., is an organization of women committed to promoting voluntarism, developing the potential of women, and improving communities through the effective action and leadership of trained volunteers. Its purpose is exclusively educational and charitable.

Library of Congress Control Number: 2004108233
ISBN: 0-9753265-0-3

Edited, Designed, and Manufactured by
Favorite Recipes® Press
an Imprint of

FRP

P. O. Box 305142
Nashville, Tennessee 37230
800-358-0560

Art Director: Steve Newman
Book Design: Starletta Polster
Project Editor: Tanis Westbrook

Manufactured in the United States of America
First Printing: 2005
10,000 copies

The Cookbook Development Committee

Amy Hopkins, *Co-Chair*
Felicia Leonard, *Co-Chair*

Art and Design
Stacey Shy, *Chair*
Cindy Forte

Marketing
Dawn M. Larson Scott, *Co-Chair*
Debbie Larson Smith, *Co-Chair*
Gwin Londrigan, *Consultant*
Debbie Boderek
Wendy Cassidy
Shannon Horrell
Heather Criss Keller
Katina Koulias
Andrea Lapenna
Andrea Ayers Layman
Monica Morris
Dina Sachs

Non-Recipe Text
Katie Cole, *Chair*
Alison Freeborn
Leona Kinnear
Christine Ruppel

Recipes
Lynne DeFilippo, *Chair*
Georgine Brancato, *Co-Chair*
Terry Banning
Cindy Brown
Zeynep DeBoer
Kandy Forenza
Nora Mihopoulos
Barbara Meyer
Rosalie Murray

Special thanks to
Jill Sketch for her research
and enthusiasm, which
led to the publication of
From Grouper to Grits.

The Board of Directors

2003-2004 President
Alison Freeborn

2004-2005 President
Jennifer McGrail

2005-2006 President
Gwin Londrigan

Executive Committee Members

Melissa Allen
Angela Breaux
Katie Cole
Deborah Cooney
Lynne DeFilippo
Carrie Durda
Laura Evans
Diane Gobo
Theresa Hess
Cory McBride
Stacey Shy

Junior League of Clearwater-Dunedin

For over fifty years, the Junior League of Clearwater-Dunedin has served the North Pinellas Community. Training women to build partnerships, inspire shared solutions, and embrace diverse perspectives, the League has worked to reach out to develop new community service organizations and help them sustain their role in the community. Your support of *From Grouper to Grits* will help us continue serving our community in the future with new partnerships and projects, similar to those we helped create throughout our history.

Community Grants

Done in a Day Projects

Dunedin Fine Art & Cultural Center

F.U.N. (Fulfilling Unique Needs) Bus

Gateway Children's Shelter

Heritage Village Historical Park

Kaleidoscope

Kids on the Block

Rick Pitino High Point Success Center

School Starts

Scot Shop

Sunshine Playground at the Long Center

UPARC/Play Parc

Jules Burt

Create. Inspire. Dream. —Jules Burt

Jules Burt has been keeping the world in full color for over a decade. Tagged as "Pop Art Diva," her inspiration for her paintings comes from her addiction to glamour and color.

Teaming with 20th Century Fox, Jules has provided set designs for the NBC series *Friends*. Several of Jules' originals have adorned America's favorite coffee house—Central Perk—on the hit series *Friends* for the past seven years, including "Fun Flower," "Glamour Queen," and the popular "Eight Cups of Coffee." Jules also provided designs for *Veronica's Closet*, *Jessie*, and *Charmed*. Her work has also appeared on NBC's *Today Show*, *Dateline NBC*, *Access Hollywood*, Oxygen Network's *She Commerce*, and CNN-FN's *Business Unusual*, as well as in a national television commercial for Wendy's Restaurants.

If you're visiting Las Vegas, check out the three cows Jules painted for the CowParade Las Vegas, 2002.

Currently, Jules has a recurring segment on WFLA-TV (NBC) called *Artrageous*. Jules is actively involved with several projects of the Outdoor Arts Foundation and sits on the Board of Directors of several area arts councils.

She says, *"It's all about believing in yourself and your work. I wake up in the morning, put on some lipstick, and conquer the day!"*

Jules Burt
www.julesburt.com
jburt3@tampabay.rr.com
tel: 813-752-2166

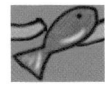

Foreword

You may have bought this cookbook in order to support the good works undertaken by this organization, and I am sure that the Junior League of Clearwater-Dunedin will put the money to proper use.

Yet, I consider a cookbook a noble thing itself. Please know that the League's efforts to assemble and publish a collection of local recipes—and your decision to purchase, read and ultimately try out a few of the recipes—are their own good works.

Cookbooks pass on the hard-won and treasured knowledge of experienced cooks, and that is more valuable today than ever.

Americans have compiled recipes, or "receipts" as Charleston still calls them, and put them in writing since colonial times. Most families in the cities and on the farms tended their own fires and cooked as their parents had, but curiosity and upward mobility drew them to written cookbooks too. In the early 1900s, professional writers and food companies began to codify basic cooking methods and recipes.

But the most intriguing can be found in the community cookbooks mimeographed and stapled together by church women and temple sister-hoods, volunteer fire departments, immigrant aid societies, and other volunteer organizations. Their recipes were more than quaint tastes of local color; they came from the real kitchens of proud cooks who had made each dish for years. Today those cookbooks are read by scholars and archived in libraries from the Culinary Institute of America to Harvard next to the most formal dissertations by chefs.

The Junior League was a leader in this tradition, providing city after city with instruction books for preserving hometown tastes.

One of them, the plastic-bound *River Road Recipes* from the Junior League of Baton Rouge that my mother bought on a vacation, was on her cookbook shelf as long as I can remember. It gave our Ohio table its first taste of gumbo, taught me "First, you make a roux," and remains to me the most authentic of Creole cookbooks.

After I left home, she was quick to send me a copy of *Cincinnati Celebrates* by the local Junior League to make sure I remembered how to make chili—and her favorite dip for parties.

On the west coast of Florida we are still defining our cuisine. As the title *From Grouper to Grits* puts it,

this collection of our cooking includes familiar Southern flavors, the fish and fruit we're known for, plus all the foods new Floridians have brought here from homes and travels across the country and around the world.

Putting such a cookbook together is not easy. As someone who has written and edited recipes for years, I know that convincing someone to share a recipe is just the start.

Ingredients and instructions must be translated from technical restaurant terms or dash-and-pinch folk wisdom, properly ordered, and proofread. (The difference between two teaspoons of baking powder and two tablespoons is explosive.)

The rest of the effort belongs to you, and it is urgent in a world that has virtually forgotten how to cook. But it is not work: use this book to enjoy cooking again.

There's an idea around that cooking is something we do for special occasions and that "party food for company" calls out our best. Perhaps, but it is cooking every day for family and friends or just for ourselves that has been lost. In the last fifty years, the convenience of frozen foods and the take-out window have sapped the cooking smarts of two or more generations.

That's a shame, and the excuse of time pressure doesn't wash. We choose how to spend time and if we decide to put it in the kitchen, we'll save money, eat better, and tailor meals to our exact dietary needs. There are few more important family gatherings. With luck and perseverance you can teach your spouse or kids to take over some cooking chores—or at least unload the dishwasher and set the table. Hey, there's no free dinner.

Maybe we'll all discover that under the rangetop, the stove has an oven. With a baking pan, a fifty-cent box of Jiffy mix, a little liquid, and thirty minutes of heat, magic will produce fresh biscuits, muffins, and corn bread. No household miracle smells so good.

Today television chefs, expensive restaurants, and trips out of town have given us a new taste for prosciutto, exotic mushrooms, and killer chocolate. Some of the recipes here will feed those tastes; others will make satisfying suppers and refreshing salads.

Somewhere in this cookbook, someone in our community has shared a recipe you'll love and cook over and over.

And pass on, I hope. Just as these good cooks have.

—*Chris Sherman*

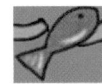

Acknowledgments

Undertaking a major cookbook was not an easy decision for the Junior League of Clearwater-Dunedin, but with the enthusiasm of our members and support of our families, we have engaged the entire community to produce this unique product. *From Grouper to Grits* is a collection of over 175 of our favorite recipes— and we know they will soon be your favorites, too. Special thanks to Jules Burt, who produced the amazing and whimsical artwork that set the stage for a new look at coastal cooking, and to her assistant, Vance Hamilton, who served as our main contact and ensured that all of the artwork was formatted correctly. Without the expertise of Chef John Lewis, La Maison Gourmet of Dunedin, our chef's tips would have been amateur guesses—thank you for your time and knowledge! Chris Sherman with the *St. Petersburg Times* donated his time, food knowledge, and writing skills to create a beautiful foreword that so expressively tells the Junior League's story. A special thanks to our husbands and families for everything from being guinea pigs, tasting unknown recipes, to filling in for car-pool shifts while we continued our stringent meeting schedule. We are also so fortunate to live in an area where so many wonderful restaurants have been born and grown to national prominence. Many donated their favorite recipes and even some money to make sure the Junior League's mission would be fulfilled. You will note the recipes from local chefs and establishments are marked at the beginning of each recipe. We only hope that you will have as much fun preparing these recipes as we did compiling them for you.

From Grouper to Grits Committee
Junior League of Clearwater-Dunedin

Introduction

Grits pl.n. *(used with a sing. or pl. verb)*
A ground, usually white meal of dried and hulled corn kernels that is boiled and served as a breakfast food or side dish; coarsely ground hulled corn boiled as a breakfast dish in the southern United States [syn: hominy grits]

Grou • per

n. pl. **grouper** or **grou • pers**

\Group"er\, n. [Corrupted fr. Pg. garupa crupper. Cf. Garbupa.] (Zo["o]l.) (a) One of several species of valuable food fishes of the genus *Epinephelus*, of the family *Serranid[ae]*, as the red grouper, or brown snapper *(E. morio)*, and the black grouper, or warsaw (*E. nigritus*), both from Florida and the Gulf of Mexico. (b) The tripletail (*Lobotes*). (c) In California, the name is often applied to the rockfishes. [Written also groper, gruper, and trooper.]

Grouper and Grits: The staple of many meals in our casual, coastal community. If a menu includes Grouper and Grits, you know you are ready for a good time. These core dishes are served formally, with sauces and specialty cheese, or casually, with some coleslaw and cold beer. Regardless of how the food is served, salt air, warm breezes, and breathtaking sunsets complement the meal.

Table of Contents

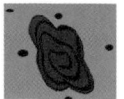

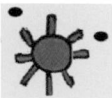

from the Sea

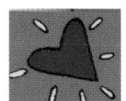

from the Side

from the Bakery

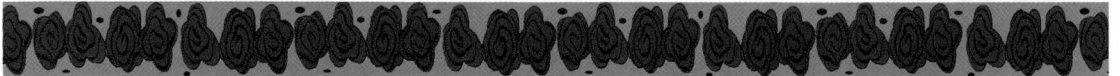

from
the
Menu

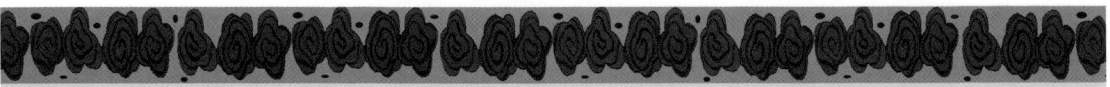

Florida Fish Fry

Baked Oysters   41
Clearwater Boil   126
Beer-Battered Fish with Bold and Spicy Tartar Sauce   109, 110
Anchovy Aïoli with Assorted Breads   54
Bacon and Blue Cheese Salad with Easy Caesar Dressing   66
Jalapeño Grits   130
Chocolate Cake with Chocolate Praline Sauce   161

From church picnics to beachside wedding parties, fish frys and oyster roasts exemplify casual entertaining. Friends and families gather on the beach, at the clubs, and in the parks among the scrub brush and cabbage palms to enjoy these local favorites. In 1949, a local judge roasted some oysters to serve to members of the Clearwater Bar Association and started a local tradition— Clearwater Bar Association's Annual Oyster Roast. Begun as a simple gathering in the orange groves where "On Top of the World" is located today, the roast now rotates to various tree-covered locales throughout the area. Served with salt and pepper, cocktail sauce, drawn butter, and crackers, this simple fare attracts thousands! Through their golden brown fried fresh fish, the Clearwater Historical Society has been passing down stories of North Pinellas heritage for many years. Each April, the Society hosts a community fish fry to celebrate Clearwater's past.

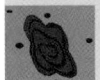

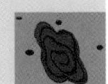

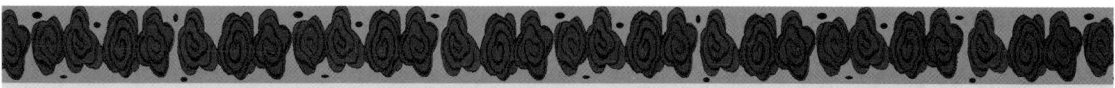

Deck the Palms for a Coastal Winter Gala

Green Bean Prosciutto Rolls   48

Grilled Sea Scallops with Roasted Red Pepper Sauce   42

Beef Tenderloin with Balsamic Sauce   86

Soft-Shell Blue Crabs with Mustard Sauce   119

Smoked Gouda Grits   130

Sweet Onion Pudding   136

Fresh Pear Salad   63

Decadent Chocolate Torte   154

Raspberry Lemon Cake   163

Winter in Florida may not bring a white Christmas, but it does bring in the stone crabs. These tasty white meat crab claws are served all winter long at gatherings from formal holiday dinners to local beach dives. By pairing these Gulf Coast treats with traditional holiday fare, hostesses create an elegant dinner with regional flair. The mild Gulf Coast weather allows many families to serve meals outdoors until January's winter showers begin. Evenings allow families to enjoy outdoor light displays that glow with our own Florida panache, including Santa's sleigh pulled by dolphins rather than reindeer, a jolly St. Nick in board shorts and sunglasses, flamingos rather than turtledoves, and evergreens covered in seashells.

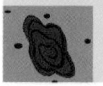
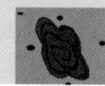

Springtime Brunch

Cocobanana Cooler   36

Sticky Bun French Toast   25

Holiday Red Apples   28

Southern Fried Grits   131

Cheese Strata   25

Homemade Waffles with Fancy Butters   26, 27

Pumpkin Coffee Cake   29

Model your spring brunch after a local favorite—UPARC's Omelette Party. When the Junior League of Clearwater-Dunedin started PlayParc in 1956, the most imaginative League member couldn't have thought that this nursery for children with disabilities would grow into the Upper Pinellas Association for Retarded Citizens—the state's largest social service agency serving mentally disabled people. Since 1967, "An Evening with Chef D'Oeuf" and "LePetit Dejeuner" have raised over two million dollars for the operations of UPARC. The menu at this black-tie evening party and morning garden party includes, of course, omelets. Rudy Stanish, "America's Omelet King," said, "Being able to make a perfect omelet is as necessary to the good life as making a good cup of coffee or tea."

"From Grouper to Grits" on the Fourth of July

Grilled Stuffed Whole Grouper   107

Firecracker Shrimp   125

Garlic Cheese Grits   28

Spinach and Avocado Salad with Toasted Walnuts   63

Basil-Marinated Grilled Vegetables   143

Tropical Delight   151

Chocolate Trifle   158

With water surrounding Pinellas County, outdoor celebrations on the boat or at the waterfront are summertime standards. Nothing beats the July Fourth celebration of fireworks illuminating the bay, rising high above Clearwater Harbor and St. Joseph's Sound. More than 10,000 residents and visitors pack Coachman Park to hear the Florida Orchestra set the stage for the majestic show. Sparkling reflections of fireworks on the water makes the display twice as spectacular. Because the fireworks are set off over the water, residents along the bay host backyard parties for friends and families to enjoy the annual celebration. Brew some homemade iced tea and start serving!

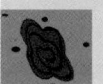
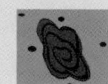

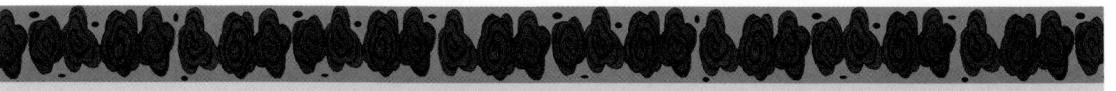

Tailgate Party

Black Olive Tapenade   53

Spicy Sweet Pecans   62

Apricot-Glazed Kielbasa   49

Mock Carpaccio   86

Spinach Salad with Creamy Garlic Dressing   65

Brown Sugar Brownies   170

Friday nights are for football in Pinellas County! High school stadiums light up the night, and the weekend tailgating begins. Saturday mornings bring heavy traffic on the roads—Interstate 75 is packed with college football fans headed north to Gainesville and Tallahassee. Florida's five Division I schools competing at the top of their conferences each year means there are plenty of tailgating cooks busy in the kitchen during the fall. With the Super Bowl™ Champion Tampa Bay Buccaneers™ just a short drive away, Sundays in the Bay area reflect the red and pewter pride.

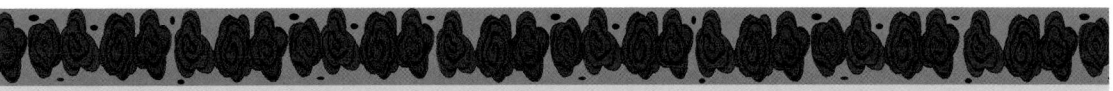

Clearwater Jazz Holiday Alfresco Supper

Vodka Breeze   38

Smoked Mullet Spread   54

Crostini with Mushrooms and Prosciutto   48

Sun-Dried Tomato and Pesto Spread   55

Cedar-Planked Shrimp   45

Spinach Salad with Hot Citrus Dressing   64

Pound Cake with Papaya Conserve   162

For 25 years, music fans have gathered at Coachman Park, overlooking the intercoastal waterway in downtown Clearwater, to hear the sounds of the Clearwater Jazz Holiday performers. Started in 1979 by the Clearwater Regional Chamber of Commerce as a way to entice travelers to our area in a slower tourist season, October's Clearwater Jazz Holiday has grown to a four-day concert, drawing over 40,000 fans annually. World-renowned jazz musicians flock to the outdoor waterfront location overlooking Clearwater's island beaches. One of the things that make the Holiday so attractive is the high-quality talent drawn to the waterfront venue—all for the cost of carrying your own blanket or chair!

Holiday Boat Parade

Bonefish Martini   37

Clearwater Cosmo   36

Sugared Cranberries   91

Cocktail Grouper Cakes with Key Lime Tartar Sauce   39

Festive Brie   51

Baked Oysters   41

Caviar Pie   52

Fresh Greens with Spicy Sweet Pecans and
Poppy Seed Dressing   62

Gruyère-Stuffed Mushrooms with Wine   50

In true seaside fashion, coastal enthusiasts celebrate the holidays with the annual Island Estates Yacht Club Holiday Boat Parade, a perfect excuse for a party or a trip to the downtown waterfront—all to watch the colorful displays and lighted boats as they cruise the intracoastal waterways between Clearwater and Dunedin. For those who don't want to join the crowds for the accompanying concert in Clearwater's Coachman Park, many hostesses open their homes for friends and families to watch the parade dockside. The parade offers an opportunity for potluck sharing and trying new holiday libations.

Sponge Docks Celebration

Sunset Margarita   37

Shrimp Cocktail with Three Sauces   46

Shrimp and Feta Cups   44

Wrapped Stuffed Dates   49

Pappas' Riverside Greek Salad   67

Grouper Piccata   105

Key Lime Pie with Macadamia Nut Crust   169

Chocolate-Crusted Amaretto Cheesecake   146

A touch of Greece is found in Tarpon Springs, home to the largest operating sponge industry outside of the Mediterranean. Dozens of boats dock at Tarpon's famous Sponge Docks. Built in 1909, the Sponge Exchange became the economic center of the community. After the industry was nearly ruined in the 1950s, two innovative brothers moved in to create the Sponge Docks as we know it today. These brothers also established Pappas' Dockside Restaurant—a landmark in the community. Each year on January 6, the Greek traditions are shown to the world through the annual Epiphany Dive for the Cross. The young Greek man who retrieves the cross, thrown by the Greek Bishop into the Spring Bayou, is said to have good luck throughout his life. Greek festivals are held at various orthodox churches through the community and always include traditional Greek specialties.

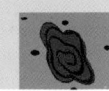

Crepes Suzette 24

Cheese Strata 25

Sticky Bun French Toast 25

Holiday Morning French Toast 26

Homemade Waffles 26

Fancy Butters 27

Holiday Red Apples 28

Garlic Cheese Grits 28

Pumpkin Coffee Cake 29

Cranberry-Nut Bread with Cream Cheese Filling 30

Macadamia Nut Bread 31

Praline Cinnamon Rolls 31

Blue Cheese Bis-grits 32

Jalapeño Corn Bread 33

Cranberry Butter 33

from
Breakfast
to
Brunch

Crepes Suzette

Serves 4

Compliments of Bon Appetit Restaurant

Crepes
1 1/2 cups flour
1 tablespoon sugar
1/2 teaspoon salt
2 cups milk
2 eggs
1/2 teaspoon vanilla extract

Orange Sauce
1/3 cup unsalted butter
2 tablespoons sugar
1/3 cup unsalted butter
2 tablespoons sugar
3/4 teaspoon grated
  orange zest
3/4 cup fresh orange juice
1/3 cup Grand Marnier
1/3 cup Curaçao

Winter on the west coast of Florida means great citrus and fresh fruit. Dr. Odet Phillippe, a Frenchman who traveled to the area to escape the Indians in Georgia, originally settled Pinellas County. He landed at present-day Phillippe Park in the mid-1830s and is credited with introducing citrus planted in rows to the world.

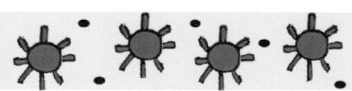

For the crepes, combine the flour, sugar, salt, milk, eggs and vanilla in a large bowl and whisk until blended. Chill, covered, for 8 hours for best results. Remove from the refrigerator and strain the batter. Melt butter to coat the bottom of a medium nonstick skillet over medium heat. Pour a small amount of the batter into the skillet. Tilt the skillet immediately to let the batter spread over the bottom of the skillet. Cook until light brown on both sides, turning once. Remove to a plate. Repeat the procedure with the remaining batter.

For the sauce, melt 1/3 cup butter in a warm pan. Add 2 tablespoons sugar and mix well. Add 1 crepe to the pan, turning to coat with the butter mixture. Fold the crepe into fourths and move to the edge of the pan. Repeat the procedure with the remaining crepes. Combine 1/3 cup butter, 2 tablespoons sugar, the orange zest and orange juice in the center of the pan and cook for 2 to 3 minutes or until heated through. Remove from the heat and add the Grand Marnier and Curaçao. Ignite and let the flames subside before serving.

Cheese Strata

Serves 12

14 slices bread
2 cups (8 ounces) shredded sharp
   Cheddar cheese
1 pound bacon, cooked and crumbled
3/4 cup (1 1/2 sticks) butter, melted

1/2 pound fresh mushrooms, sliced
7 eggs
3 1/2 cups milk
2 teaspoons prepared mustard
1/2 teaspoon salt

Trim the crusts from the bread and cut the bread into cubes. Arrange half the bread cubes in a 9×13-inch baking dish. Sprinkle with half the cheese and half the bacon. Drizzle with half the butter. Repeat the layers and top with the mushrooms.

Beat the eggs, milk, mustard and salt in a bowl until blended. Pour over the prepared dish. Chill, covered, for 8 hours. Bake at 300 degrees for 90 minutes.

 **Chef's Tip:** Replace the bacon with cooked and crumbled medium or spicy sausage for a different taste.

Sticky Bun French Toast

Serves 6 to 8

1 loaf French bread, cut into
   1-inch slices
6 eggs
1 1/2 cups milk
1 1/2 cups half-and-half
1 teaspoon vanilla extract

1/4 teaspoon cinnamon
1/8 teaspoon nutmeg
1/2 cup (1 stick) butter or margarine
1 cup packed brown sugar
2 tablespoons dark corn syrup
1/2 cup chopped nuts

Arrange the bread slices in a single layer in a buttered 9×13-inch baking dish. Process the next 6 ingredients in a blender until smooth. Pour over the bread layer. Chill, covered, for 8 hours. Remove from the refrigerator and let stand at room temperature for 30 minutes or longer. Melt the butter in a small saucepan over medium heat. Add the brown sugar and corn syrup and mix well. Stir in the nuts. Spread over the prepared dish. Bake at 350 degrees for 40 to 50 minutes or until puffed and golden brown. Serve with maple syrup.

Holiday Morning French Toast

Serves 12

1 cup packed brown sugar
1/2 cup (1 stick) butter, melted
1 teaspoon cinnamon
3 tart apples, peeled and
   thinly sliced
1/2 cup dried cranberries

1 loaf Italian or French bread,
   cut into 1-inch slices
6 eggs
1 1/2 cups milk
1 tablespoon vanilla extract
2 teaspoons cinnamon

Combine the brown sugar, butter and 1 teaspoon cinnamon in a bowl and mix well. Add the apples and cranberries and toss to coat. Spoon the mixture evenly over the bottom of a 9×13-inch baking dish. Arrange the bread slices over the top of the apple mixture. Combine the eggs, milk, vanilla and 2 teaspoons cinnamon in a bowl and beat until blended. Pour over the bread layer. Chill, covered, for 8 hours. Bake, covered with foil, at 375 degrees for 40 minutes. Bake, uncovered, for 5 minutes. Remove from the oven and let stand for 5 minutes before serving.

 **Chef's Tip:** To prevent dried fruits from sticking to the knife blade, spray the knife blade with cooking spray or coat with vegetable oil.

Homemade Waffles

Serves 8

1 1/2 cups milk
2 eggs
2 cups flour

3 teaspoons baking powder
2 teaspoons sugar
1/2 cup (1 stick) butter, melted

Combine the milk, eggs, flour, baking powder and sugar in a blender and process until smooth. Add the butter and process until blended. Pour 1/3 cup batter onto a hot waffle iron. Bake until golden brown. Serve with your choice of fancy butter, maple syrup, fresh fruit or granola and whipped cream.

Fancy Butters

Praline Butter
1/2 cup sugar
1/3 cup water
1/2 cup chopped pecans
3/4 cup (1 1/2 sticks) butter, softened

Orange Honey Butter
1/2 cup (1 stick) unsalted butter,
   at room temperature
2 tablespoons honey
1 tablespoon grated orange zest

Raspberry Butter
1/2 cup (1 stick) butter, softened
1/2 cup crushed raspberries
1 tablespoon sugar, or 1/4 cup
   raspberry jam

For the praline butter, combine the sugar and water in a saucepan over medium heat and stir until the sugar dissolves. Cook for 8 to 10 minutes or until the mixture reaches 300 degrees on a candy thermometer and is amber-colored. Do not stir. Remove from the heat and stir in the pecans. Pour onto a buttered baking sheet. Let stand for 10 to 15 minutes or until cool. Break the praline into pieces and place in a food processor. Process until a coarse powder consistency. Combine with the butter in a small bowl and mix well. This may be prepared several days in advance and stored in the refrigerator. Bring to room temperature before serving.

For the orange honey butter, beat the butter in a small bowl until light and fluffy. Add the honey and orange zest and beat until blended.

For the raspberry butter, combine the butter, raspberries and sugar in a small bowl and beat until blended. You may substitute strawberries and strawberry jam for the raspberries and raspberry jam if preferred.

Holiday Red Apples

Serves 6

    1 cup water
    8 ounces red hot cinnamon candies
    6 Granny Smith apples, peeled and cored
    6 cinnamon sticks

Combine the water and candies in a large saucepan over medium heat and cook until the candies melt and the mixture thickens, stirring constantly. Place the apples in the pan. Place a cinnamon stick in the center of each apple. Reduce the heat to low and cook, covered, for 30 minutes or until the apples are softened and bright red, basting with the candy syrup occasionally. Remove the apples to a serving dish and spoon the candy syrup over the apples. Refrigerate until the apples are chilled.

Garlic Cheese Grits

Serves 8 to 10

    4 cups water
    1 teaspoon salt
    1 cup grits
    2 to 3 garlic cloves, minced
    1/2 cup (1 stick) butter

3/4 pound Velveeta cheese
2 eggs, beaten
milk
1 cup (4 ounces) shredded
    Cheddar cheese

Combine the water and salt in a saucepan and bring to a boil. Stir in the grits and garlic. Reduce the heat and cook until thickened, stirring frequently. Remove from the heat. Add the butter and Velveeta cheese and stir until melted. Add enough milk to the eggs to measure 1 cup. Pour into the grits and mix well. Spoon the mixture into a baking dish. Bake at 350 degrees for 45 minutes. Sprinkle with the Cheddar cheese and bake until the cheese is melted.

Chef's Tip: Cut leftover grits into squares, dust with flour, and sauté in butter for the next day's treat!

Pumpkin Coffee Cake

Serves 12

Filling
1 (16-ounce) can pumpkin
1 egg
1/3 cup sugar
1 teaspoon cinnamon
1/2 teaspoon ginger
1/2 teaspoon nutmeg
1/4 teaspoon allspice
1/4 teaspoon cloves

Streusel Topping
1 cup packed brown sugar
2 tablespoons flour
2 teaspoons cinnamon
1/3 cup butter, chopped
1 cup chopped walnuts

Cake
1/2 cup (1 stick) butter, softened
3/4 cup sugar
1 teaspoon vanilla extract
3 eggs
2 cups flour
1 teaspoon baking powder
1 teaspoon baking soda
1 cup sour cream

For the filling, combine the pumpkin, egg, sugar, cinnamon, ginger, nutmeg, allspice and cloves in a bowl and mix well.

For the topping, combine the brown sugar, flour and cinnamon in a bowl and mix well. Cut in the butter until crumbly. Add the walnuts and toss to mix.

For the cake, cream the butter, sugar and vanilla in a bowl until light and fluffy. Add the eggs 1 at a time, beating well after each addition. Sift the flour, baking powder and baking soda together in a bowl. Add to the creamed mixture alternately with the sour cream, mixing well after each addition.

Pour half the cake batter into a greased 9×13-inch baking pan. Sprinkle with half the streusel mixture. Spread the filling evenly over the top. Top with the remaining cake batter and sprinkle with the remaining streusel mixture. Bake at 325 degrees for 50 minutes.

Cranberry-Nut Bread with Cream Cheese Filling

Makes 1 loaf

The Junior League of Clearwater and the Junior Service League of Dunedin joined forces in 1986 to create the Junior League of Clearwater-Dunedin. Since then, more than $500,000 has been given back to the community. Tracking investments since the Junior League of Clearwater started in 1948 brings that total to more than $1.3 million.

8 ounces cream cheese, softened
1 egg
1/3 cup sugar
1 tablespoon flour
boiling water
juice of 1 orange
grated zest of 1 orange
2 tablespoons butter or margarine

1 cup sugar
1 egg
1 cup chopped cranberries
1/2 cup chopped nuts
2 cups flour
1/2 teaspoon baking soda
1/2 teaspoon salt

Combine the cream cheese, 1 egg, 1/3 cup sugar and 1 tablespoon flour in a mixing bowl and beat until blended.

Combine enough boiling water and orange juice to measure 3/4 cup. Add the orange zest and butter and mix well. Combine 1 cup sugar and 1 egg in a mixing bowl and beat well. Add to the orange mixture and mix well. Stir in the cranberries and nuts. Sift 2 cups flour, the baking soda and salt together in a bowl. Add to the orange mixture and mix well.

Pour 2/3 of the batter into a greased 5×9-inch loaf pan. Pour the cream cheese mixture over the center of the batter. Pour the remaining 1/3 of the batter over the filling. Bake at 325 degrees for 1 hour. Cool in the pan for 15 minutes. Remove to a wire rack to cool completely. For best results, do not slice the bread for 8 hours.

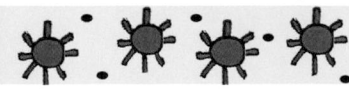

Macadamia Nut Bread

Makes 2 loaves

1/2 cup sour cream
2 teaspoons baking soda
3 to 4 ripe bananas, mashed
4 medium eggs, beaten
1 cup (2 sticks) butter, softened
2 teaspoons vanilla extract
3 cups sifted flour

2 cups sugar
2 pinches salt
1/2 cup coarsely chopped
   macadamia nuts
1/2 cup coarsely chopped fresh
   cranberries (optional)

Combine the sour cream and baking soda in a bowl and mix well. Combine the bananas, eggs, butter and vanilla in a large mixing bowl and beat until blended. Add the flour, sugar, salt and sour cream mixture and mix well. Stir in the macadamia nuts and cranberries.

Spoon into 2 greased and floured loaf pans. Bake at 350 degrees for 35 to 40 minutes or until a wooden pick inserted in the center comes out clean.

Hint: Save one of the loaves to eat later by freezing it. When freezing bread, double-wrap tightly in plastic wrap and place in a sealable freezer bag with the description and date marked on the bag. The bread will keep for up to two months.

Praline Cinnamon Rolls

Serves 10

1 loaf frozen bread dough, thawed
3 tablespoons butter, softened
3/4 cup packed brown sugar

3 teaspoons cinnamon
3/4 cup pecan halves
6 tablespoons dark corn syrup

Roll the bread dough out to a 1/4-inch-thick rectangle. Spread the butter over the bread dough and sprinkle with the brown sugar and cinnamon. Roll as for a jelly roll. Cut into 3/4-inch slices. Sprinkle the pecans over the bottom of a well greased round baking dish. Arrange the dough slices over the top. Pour the corn syrup over the dough. Let rise until doubled in size. Bake at 350 degrees for 30 minutes. Let stand for 5 minutes. Invert onto a platter.

Blue Cheese Bis-grits

2 cups flour
1 teaspoon sugar
1 teaspoon salt
2 teaspoons baking powder
1/2 teaspoon baking soda
1/4 cup (1/2 stick) butter

1/2 cup cooked grits, cooled
1/4 cup buttermilk
4 ounces blue cheese, crumbled
6 tablespoons butter

Real stone-ground grits require preparation, including rinsing to separate the last remains of the hull, or chaff, from the kernel. To do this, cover the grits with cold water, skim the chaff off the surface, and drain. To prepare the grits, bring 4 cups water to a boil in a medium saucepan. Add 1/2 teaspoon salt and slowly stir in 1 cup stone-ground grits. Simmer for 40 minutes or until the grits are thick and creamy, stirring frequently. Remove from the heat and stir in 2 tablespoons unsalted butter. Serve immediately.

Sift the flour, sugar, salt, baking powder and baking soda together into a bowl. Cut in 1/4 cup butter until crumbly. Combine the grits and buttermilk in a mixing bowl and beat until smooth. Stir in the flour mixture. Turn out onto a floured surface and knead 12 to 15 times.

Pat the dough to a 1/2-inch thickness. Cut into 2-inch rounds and arrange in a greased baking dish. Combine the cheese and 6 tablespoons butter in a small saucepan over medium heat and cook until the cheese is melted, stirring frequently. Pour over the prepared dish. Bake at 350 degrees for 10 minutes.

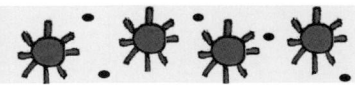

Jalapeño Corn Bread

Serves 6 to 8

2 cups flour
1 tablespoon baking powder
3/4 teaspoon salt
1 cup cornmeal
3/4 cup sugar

2 eggs, beaten
1 1/2 cups milk
1 tablespoon butter, melted
2 tablespoons chopped seeded
  jalapeño chiles

Sift the flour, baking powder and salt together into a large bowl. Add the cornmeal and mix well. Combine the sugar and eggs in a bowl and beat until blended. Beat in the milk, butter and flour mixture. Stir in the jalapeño chiles. Pour into a buttered 8×9-inch baking dish. Bake at 400 degrees for 20 minutes.

Cranberry Butter

Serves 16

1/2 cup dried sweetened cranberries
1 1/2 cups orange juice
1 cup (2 sticks) butter, softened
3 tablespoons confectioners' sugar

Combine the cranberries and orange juice in a small saucepan over medium heat and bring to a simmer. Remove from the heat and let stand for 20 minutes. Strain the cranberries. Place in a food processor and pulse until finely chopped. Combine with the butter and confectioners' sugar in a bowl and mix well. Spoon into butter molds or small ramekins and chill until ready to use. Serve with corn bread muffins or toast.

Clearwater Cosmo 36

Cocobanana Cooler 36

Sunset Margarita 37

Bonefish Martini 37

Vodka Breeze 38

The Columbia's Sangria de Cava 38

Cocktail Grouper Cakes with
Key Lime Tartar Sauce 39

Crab Canapés 40

Baked Oysters 41

Grilled Jumbo Atlantic Sea Scallops
with Roasted Red Pepper Sauce 42

Sea Scallops Over Corn Cakes 43

Shrimp and Feta Cups 44

Cedar-Planked Shrimp 45

Shrimp Cocktail with Three Sauces 46

Fresh Tomato Basil Bruschetta 47

Crostini with Mushrooms
and Prosciutto 48

Green Bean Prosciutto Rolls 48

Apricot-Glazed Kielbasa 49

Wrapped Stuffed Dates 49

Gruyère-Stuffed Mushrooms
with Wine 50

Peppers Provençal 51

Festive Brie 51

Caviar Pie 52

Black Olive Tapenade 53

Hot Ham Spread with Savory Pecans 53

Anchovy Aïoli 54

Smoked Fish Spread 54

Sun-Dried Tomato and
Pesto Spread 55

Fresh Three-Pepper Salsa 55

Santorini Salsa 56

Chunky Avocado Dip 57

Holy Guacamole! 58

Pita Chips 58

Mediterranean Dip 59

Vidalia Onion Cheese Dip 59

from the
Beginning

Clearwater Cosmo

Serves 1

¼ cup cranberry-raspberry juice
2 tablespoons Vodka
2 tablespoons Rose's sweetened
    lime juice

2 tablespoons Triple Sec or
    Grand Marnier
1½ cups cracked ice

Combine the cranberry-raspberry juice, Vodka, lime juice, Triple Sec and ice in a cocktail shaker and shake well to combine. Strain into a glass. Garnish with a lime wedge.

Cocobanana Cooler

Makes about 13 cups

6 ripe bananas, sliced
1 cup lemon juice
2 cups light cream
1 cup sugar

42 ounces lemon-lime soda
1 pint lemon sherbet
⅓ cup flaked coconut

Purée the bananas and lemon juice in a blender. Combine with the cream and sugar in a large container. Chill until ready to serve. To serve, combine with the soda in a pitcher or punch bowl and stir gently to blend. Ladle into punch cups or stemmed glasses. Top each with a spoonful of the sherbet and a sprinkle of the coconut.

 **Chef's Tip:** Add rum to create an adult's tropical party drink!

Sunset Margarita

Serves 4

1 (12-ounce) can light beer
1 (12-ounce) can frozen
   limeade concentrate, thawed

12 ounces water
12 ounces Tequila
6 ounces Triple Sec (optional)

Combine the beer, limeade concentrate, water, Tequila and Triple Sec in a pitcher and stir gently to mix. Serve over ice. For frozen margaritas, process the mixture with ice in a blender until slushy.

Hint: Rub lime around the rim of a glass and dip the glass in margarita salt. Add a lime wedge to the glass.

Bonefish Martini

Serves 1

Special thanks to Bonefish Grill for sharing this award-winning martini recipe.

1 1/4 ounces high-quality
   Vodka
1 ounce cranberry juice
dry Champagne

Combine the Vodka and cranberry juice with ice in a cocktail shaker and shake well to mix. Strain into a martini glass. Pour in Champagne to fill the glass. Garnish with an orange slice.

Every evening, two hours before and after sunset, artisans, street performers, musicians, and others take over the activity center of Clearwater to celebrate the setting of the sun. This family-oriented tradition was voted the Second Best Sunset in the state (only Key West ranked higher) according to Florida Monthly readers.

Vodka Breeze

Makes about 3 quarts

3 cups sugar
1 cup water
1 1/3 cups fresh lemon juice

zest of 4 lemons
2 quarts ice water
1 1/2 to 2 cups Vodka

Combine the sugar and 1 cup water in a small saucepan over medium heat. Bring the mixture to a boil, stirring constantly. Reduce the heat and simmer for 5 minutes, stirring occasionally. Remove from the heat and let stand until cool. Combine the sugar mixture, lemon juice, lemon zest, 2 quarts ice water and Vodka in a pitcher and stir gently to mix. Let stand for 10 minutes. Remove the lemon zest. Serve over crushed ice and garnish with mint sprigs.

Hint: Zest is the colored part of the skin of any citrus fruit. When grating zest, use a small grater or zester to get the maximum result.

The Columbia's Sangria de Cava

Serves 2

The Columbia Restaurant, a community favorite for Spanish specialties, is Florida's oldest restaurant. Continuously operated by the Gonzmart family, the Columbia has six locations throughout Florida, including Clearwater Beach and the original location in Ybor City.

1/2 (750-milliliter) bottle
   Freixenet Semi-Sec
7 ounces lemon-lime soda

3/4 ounce simple syrup
1 1/4 ounces orange liqueur
1 1/4 ounces Brandy

Combine the Semi-Sec, soda, simple syrup, orange liqueur and Brandy in a pitcher and mix well. Chill until ready to serve. Pour into glasses and garnish with an orange slice, lime slice and cherry.

Freixenet is not a "Champagne," as it is not produced in the region of Champagne in France according to the strict specifications allowing that labeling. Freixenet is actually a sparkling wine produced in Spain. Semi-Secco (or Semi-Sec) pleases most palates, as it has a good mix of sweetness and spiciness and tends to be fruitier in taste than brut.

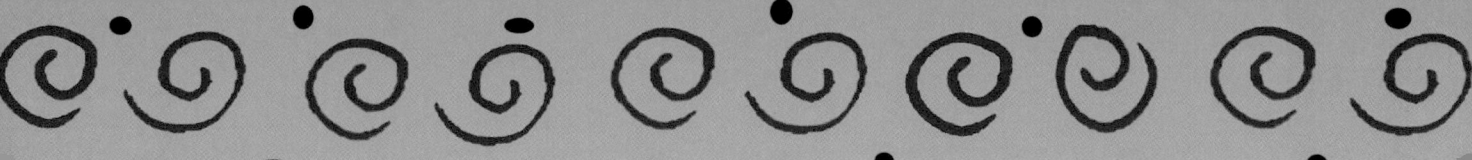

Cocktail Grouper Cakes with Key Lime Tartar Sauce

Serves 8 to 10

Black Cat Gourmet To Go Catering generously shares this grouper recipe.

1 pound grouper
1/8 teaspoon Old Bay Seasoning
1 small onion, minced
1 scallion, minced
1 rib celery, minced
1/4 green bell pepper, finely chopped
1/4 cup chopped fresh parsley
1 cup fresh white bread crumbs
1 egg, beaten
1/2 cup mayonnaise
1/2 teaspoon Dijon mustard
1/8 teaspoon Worcestershire sauce

1/2 teaspoon thyme
pinch of cayenne pepper
salt and black pepper to taste
1 egg
1 tablespoon water
1 cup fresh white bread crumbs
1 cup mayonnaise
1/2 cup sour cream
1 teaspoon key lime juice
1/4 cup capers
2 tablespoons chopped fresh parsley
margarine

Combine the grouper and Old Bay Seasoning with simmering water to cover in a saucepan. Poach just until the grouper is white. Drain and rinse with cool water. Crumble the fish into a large bowl. Add the onion, scallion, celery, bell pepper, parsley, 1 cup bread crumbs, egg, 1/2 cup mayonnaise, mustard, Worcestershire sauce, thyme, cayenne pepper, salt and black pepper and mix well. Shape into small patties.

Whisk together the egg and water in a shallow dish. Dip the patties in the egg mixture and roll in 1 cup bread crumbs. Arrange on a tray and chill, covered, for 6 to 8 hours. Combine 1 cup mayonnaise, the sour cream, key lime juice, capers and parsley in a bowl and mix well. Chill until ready to serve. Sauté the patties in margarine in a skillet over medium heat until golden and puffed, turning once. Serve with the sauce.

Chef's Tip: This also makes a great Florida meal. The grouper cakes may be made in advance and reheated in a 250-degree oven for about 10 minutes.

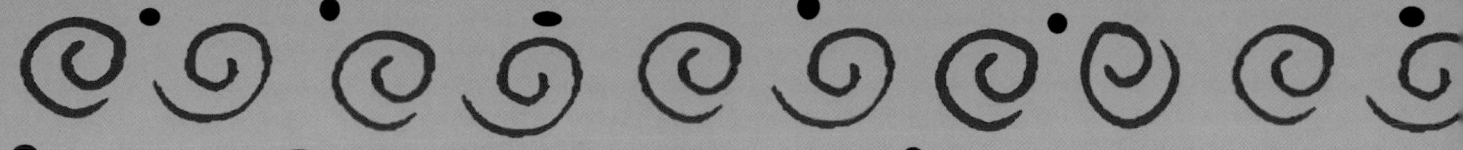

Crab Canapés

Makes 48 canapés

2 (8-count) packages
  refrigerator butterflake
  biscuits
1 pound fresh lump
  crab meat
12 ounces cream cheese,
  softened
1/4 cup mayonnaise
1 cup (4 ounces) shredded
  Cheddar cheese

1/4 cup (1 ounce) grated
  Parmesan cheese
1/4 cup minced shallots
2 teaspoons Worcestershire
  sauce
seasoned salt to taste
pepper to taste
paprika

Separate each biscuit into 3 layers. Press each layer into a miniature muffin cup. Combine the crab meat, cream cheese, mayonnaise, Cheddar cheese, Parmesan cheese, shallots, Worcestershire sauce, seasoned salt and pepper in a bowl and mix well.

Place 1 tablespoon of the crab mixture into each prepared muffin cup. Sprinkle with paprika. Bake at 375 degrees for 15 minutes or until light brown. Let cool for 5 minutes.

Chef's Tip: These may be prepared in advance and frozen until ready to serve. Reheat at 375 degrees for 15 minutes.

Baked Oysters

Serves 6

1/4 cup (1/2 stick) butter
1/4 cup olive oil
2/3 cup bread crumbs
1/4 cup (1 ounce) grated
   Parmesan cheese
2 tablespoons finely chopped
   green onions
2 tablespoons chopped
   fresh parsley

2 teaspoons minced garlic
1/2 teaspoon oregano
1/2 teaspoon tarragon
1/2 teaspoon salt
1/2 teaspoon black pepper
1/8 teaspoon cayenne pepper
2 1/2 to 3 dozen oysters

Heat the butter and olive oil in a saucepan over medium heat for 2 minutes. Remove from the heat and stir in the bread crumbs, Parmesan cheese, green onions, parsley, garlic, oregano, tarragon, salt, black pepper and cayenne pepper. Arrange the oysters in a 9-inch disposable baking dish. Spoon the bread crumb mixture over the oysters. Bake at 450 degrees for 12 to 16 minutes or until the top is brown. Serve immediately with toast points.

An old wives' tale says that you should eat oysters only in months ending with the letter "r" to make sure the water temperature is cool enough. It is good timing in the Gulf of Mexico, as those months that are off-limits for oysters offer other local delicacies, like Florida spiny lobster and spring's end of stone crab season.

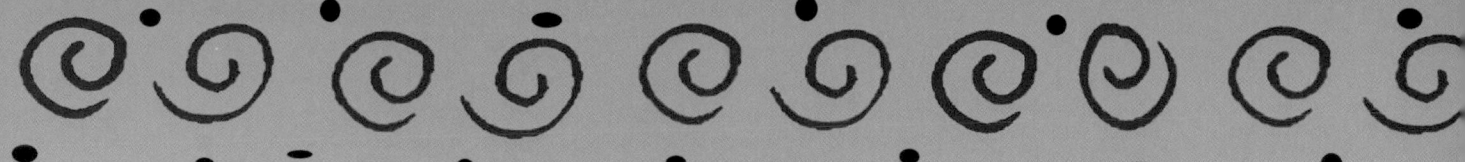

Grilled Jumbo Atlantic Sea Scallops with Roasted Red Pepper Sauce

Serves 4

Chef Daniel Fuchs shares his favorite appetizer from the Clearwater Beach Hotel.

1 cup olive oil
juice of ¹/₂ lemon
juice of ¹/₂ lime
3 garlic cloves
2 scallions, chopped
1 sprig each of rosemary,
   dill weed and basil
1 teaspoon coarsely ground
   pepper

8 (2-ounce) sea scallops
1 red bell pepper
1 tablespoon chopped shallot
3 tablespoons dry white wine
1 cup heavy cream
salt and freshly ground
   pepper to taste
4 ounces smoked salmon,
   cut into 8 slices

The Clearwater Beach Hotel, the centerpiece of Clearwater Beach for over 40 years, offers fine dining, a tradition of hospitality, and a combination of casual, kick-off-your-shoes fun with the grandeur of the sprawling property. The historic nature of the property makes it popular for wedding showers and receptions.

Mix the olive oil, lemon juice, lime juice, garlic, scallions, rosemary, dill weed, basil and pepper in a bowl. Place the scallops in the marinade and marinate in the refrigerator for 3 hours.

Grill the bell pepper over high heat until the skin is black, turning frequently. Remove the bell pepper from the grill and place in a brown paper bag. Let stand for 10 minutes. Remove the blackened skin. Cut the bell pepper in half and remove the seeds. Purée the bell pepper in a food processor.

Combine the shallot with the wine in a skillet over medium heat. Cook until most of the liquid has evaporated, stirring frequently. Add the cream and cook until reduced by half, stirring frequently. Add the puréed bell pepper, salt and pepper to taste and mix well.

Drain the scallops, discarding the marinade. Wrap each scallop with a slice of salmon and secure with a wooden pick. Grill the prepared scallops over medium-high heat for 1 to 3 minutes per side. Serve over roasted red pepper sauce. Garnish with sour cream and caviar.

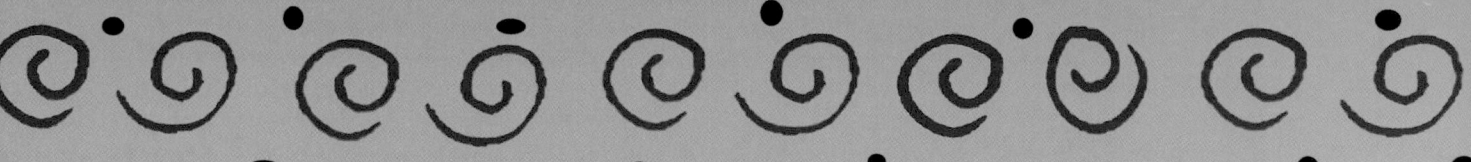

Sea Scallops Over Corn Cakes

olive oil
12 large sea scallops
3 tablespoons olive oil
2 tablespoons chopped garlic
1/4 cup balsamic vinegar
salt and pepper to taste
1 (8-ounce) package corn bread mix
vegetable oil

Heat a small amount of olive oil in a skillet over medium heat. Add the scallops and sauté until most of the liquid is released. Drain or cook until the liquid has evaporated. Add 3 tablespoons olive oil and the garlic and sauté until the flavors are released and the scallops are fully cooked. Drizzle with the balsamic vinegar. Season with salt and pepper.

Prepare the corn bread mix using the package directions, reducing the amount of liquid for a thicker consistency. Heat vegetable oil in a sauté pan. Pour 1/4 cup of the corn bread mixture into the pan and cook until the edges are bubbly and the bottom is golden. Turn over the corn cake and cook until golden on the other side. Remove to a paper towel-lined plate to drain. Repeat the procedure with the remaining corn bread mixture.

To serve, place 3 scallops on each corn cake. Drizzle with the balsamic vinegar sauce from the skillet.

 **Chef's Tip:** Create a touch of elegance by adding some corn kernels to your batter/cakes.

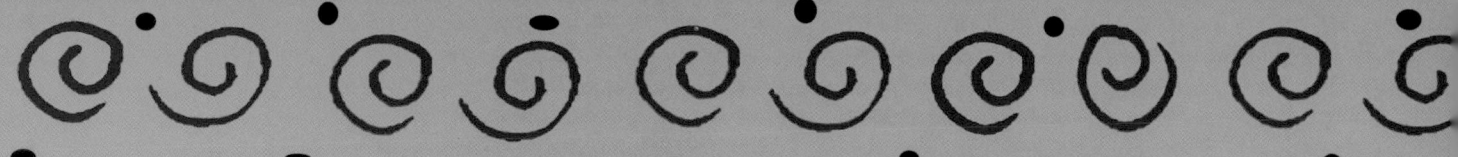

Shrimp and Feta Cups

Serves 24

8 ounces white mushroom caps, finely chopped
5 to 8 ounces shrimp, cooked, peeled and deveined
4 ounces feta cheese, crumbled
1 egg, lightly beaten
24 unbaked tart shells

Sauté the mushrooms in a nonstick skillet over medium heat until tender; drain. Chop the shrimp. Combine with the cheese, egg and mushrooms in a bowl and mix well. Arrange the tart shells on a baking sheet. Spoon the mushroom mixture into the tart shells. Bake at 350 degrees for 12 to 15 minutes or until golden brown.

Chef's Tip: Substitute pre-made phyllo dough cups, available at Greek marketplaces, for the tart shells. This adds a wonderful Mediterranean taste.

Heritage Village, in Largo, a turn-of-the century living history museum where men and women dress in period costume, found its beginnings as a Junior League project in conjunction with the county and the Historical Society. Today, more than 100,000 people per year visit the village to learn about the history of Pinellas County.

Cedar-Planked Shrimp

Serves 6 to 8

3 to 4 pieces fresh gingerroot,
  thinly sliced
2 to 4 garlic cloves, finely minced
1/2 cup soy sauce

1/4 cup dry sherry
1/4 cup olive oil
1 pound shrimp, tails on, peeled
  and deveined

Submerge a 1-inch-thick 12-inch-square cedar plank in water and let soak for
30 minutes or longer. Combine the gingerroot, garlic, soy sauce, sherry and olive
oil in a bowl and mix well. Add the shrimp and stir gently to coat. Marinate in
the refrigerator for 1 hour. To prevent the shrimp from becoming mushy, do not
marinate for longer than 1 hour. Drain the shrimp and discard the marinade.

Remove the cedar plank from the water. Arrange the shrimp on the cedar
plank. Grill over high heat for 10 minutes or until the shrimp are done. Do not
turn the shrimp. Serve immediately or at room temperature. Serve with your
favorite sauce or salsa. You may substitute chicken or fish for the shrimp if
preferred. If cooking fish, leave the skin on 1 side of the fish and place it skin
side down on the cedar plank.

 **Chef's Tip:** Next time, try soaking the cedar plank in white wine or beer
for a different, pleasing flavor. Place a brick or something heavy on the
cedar plank to make sure that it stays fully submerged.

Shrimp Cocktail with Three Sauces

Serves 2 to 4

Shrimp
2 to 3 bay leaves
1 teaspoon whole peppercorns
1 pound (21- to 30-count) shrimp

Spicy Cocktail Sauce
$1/2$ cup ketchup
1 tablespoon horseradish, or to taste
4 drops Worcestershire sauce
juice of $1/4$ lemon
pepper to taste

Curry Aïoli Sauce
1 cup mayonnaise
1 tablespoon lemon juice
1 teaspoon sugar
1 to 3 tablespoons curry powder, or
   to taste
salt and pepper to taste

Horseradish Mustard Sauce
$1/2$ cup Dijon mustard
$1/4$ cup sour cream
$1/4$ to $1/3$ cup horseradish, drained
pepper to taste

For the shrimp, fill a 2-gallon stockpot with water and add the bay leaves and peppercorns. Bring to a boil. Add the shrimp and boil for 2 minutes or until the shrimp turn pink. Drain and rinse immediately with cold water to stop the cooking process. Let cool for 15 minutes. Peel and devein the shrimp, leaving the tails on. Chill, covered, for 1 hour.

For the cocktail sauce, combine the ketchup, horseradish, Worcestershire sauce, lemon juice and pepper in a bowl and whisk until blended. Chill, covered, until ready to serve.

For the aïoli sauce, combine the mayonnaise, lemon juice, sugar, curry powder, salt and pepper in a bowl and mix well. Chill, covered, until ready to serve.

For the mustard sauce, combine the mustard, sour cream and horseradish in a bowl and mix well. Season with pepper. Chill, covered, until ready to serve.

To serve, arrange the shrimp on a chilled serving platter. Garnish with fresh greens and lemon wedges. Serve with the sauces on the side.

For a beautiful presentation of cold shrimp, try these tips: To wash and clean shrimp, remove the shell, keeping the tail attached. To make the shrimp extra cold, put in the freezer for five minutes before serving, fill a serving dish with crushed or cracked ice, and arrange the shrimp over the ice.

Fresh Tomato Basil Bruschetta   Serves 10 to 12

2¹/2 pounds plum tomatoes,
   seeded and chopped
¹/4 teaspoon kosher salt
1 French baguette, cut into
   ¹/4-inch slices
olive oil
3 to 4 garlic cloves, minced
¹/2 cup finely chopped onion

2 tablespoons chopped
   fresh basil
¹/4 teaspoon sugar
1 tablespoon olive oil
1 teaspoon balsamic vinegar
kosher salt to taste
freshly ground pepper
   to taste

Place the tomatoes in a colander over the sink. Sprinkle with
¹/4 teaspoon kosher salt. Let drain for 2 hours or longer. Arrange
the baguette slices on a foil-lined baking sheet. Brush with olive
oil. Bake at 375 degrees for 8 to 10 minutes or until lightly toasted.

   Combine the tomatoes, garlic, onion, basil, sugar, 1 tablespoon
olive oil and balsamic vinegar in a bowl and mix gently. Season
with kosher salt and pepper to taste. Top each baguette slice
with 1 to 2 teaspoons of the tomato mixture. Garnish with fresh
basil leaves.

   Hint: To easily seed a whole tomato, cut it in half horizontally.
Squeeze each half to loosen the seeds. Hold the tomato half cut
side down over the garbage can and shake vigorously.

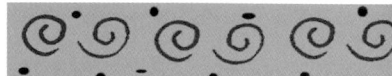

*Fort DeSoto, a
Spanish-American
War fort, towers
over the pass in
southern Pinellas
County. Visitors
to the island can
still climb the
batteries and
visualize what
happened in
the 1800s.*

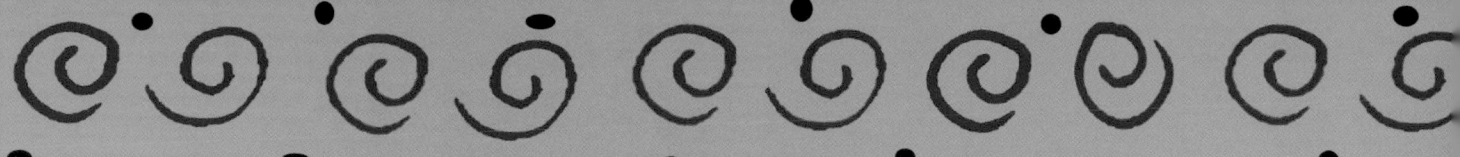

Crostini with Mushrooms and Prosciutto

Serves 18

3 tablespoons butter
8 ouncees shiitake mushrooms, chopped
4 ounces cremini mushrooms, chopped
2 garlic cloves, minced
1/2 cup heavy cream

1/2 cup (2 ounces) crumbled blue cheese
1/2 cup chopped prosciutto
salt and pepper to taste
18 (1/4-inch-thick) sourdough baguette slices
chopped fresh parsley

Melt the butter in a large skillet over medium-high heat. Add the mushrooms and garlic and cook for 10 minutes or until brown, stirring frequently. Add the cream and bring to a boil. Boil for 2 minutes or until the liquid is absorbed, stirring frequently. Remove from the heat. Add the cheese and stir until melted. Add the prosciutto and mix well. Season with salt and pepper.

Arrange the baguette slices on a baking sheet. Bake at 375 degrees until golden brown. Top each slice with 1 tablespoon of the mushroom mixture. Bake at 375 degrees for 6 minutes or until heated through. Sprinkle with parsley.

Green Bean Prosciutto Rolls

Serves 20

1 pound fresh green beans, trimmed
1/2 ounce fresh basil leaves
1/4 cup grated Romano cheese

3/4 pound prosciutto, sliced
2 tablespoons grated Romano cheese
1/4 teaspoon olive oil

Combine the green beans with boiling water to cover in a saucepan and boil for 2 minutes. Plunge immediately into ice water to stop the cooking process; drain. Place 3 to 4 green beans, 1 basil leaf, and 1/8 teaspoon cheese on 1 slice prosciutto. Roll up the prosciutto to enclose. Repeat the procedure with the remaining green beans, basil, 1/4 cup cheese and prosciutto. Arrange on a serving dish. Sprinkle with 2 tablespoons cheese and drizzle with the olive oil.

Hint: When trimming green beans, cut off only the end that was attached to the plant. The other end is edible.

Apricot-Glazed Kielbasa

Serves 6 to 8

Kielbasa may spawn memories of football played in snow and shivering tailgaters. But even in Florida, the food remains a great Super Bowl party appetizer.

1 cup apricot preserves	1 tablespoon Dijon mustard
1/4 cup blackberry preserves	1 teaspoon ginger
2 tablespoons lemon juice	1 1/2 pounds kielbasa, sliced

Combine the apricot preserves, blackberry preserves, lemon juice, mustard and ginger in a small bowl and mix well. Cook the kielbasa in a large skillet over medium heat for 3 minutes, turning often. Add the apricot mixture and cook for 8 minutes or until heated through, stirring occasionally. Serve immediately.

 **Chef's Tip:** Serve over rice pilaf for a main dish.

Wrapped Stuffed Dates

Serves 10 to 12

1 pound bacon
1 1/2 cups unsalted whole almonds
8 ounces dates

Cut each bacon slice in half. Insert an almond in each date. Wrap 1 piece of bacon around each prepared date and secure with a wooden pick. Arrange in a single layer on a baking sheet. Broil until brown on both sides, turning once. Remove to a paper towel to drain. Let stand for 2 minutes before serving.

Gruyère-Stuffed Mushrooms with Wine

Serves 24

1 onion, finely chopped
2 tablespoons olive oil
24 mushrooms, stems removed and
  finely chopped
1/4 cup finely chopped fresh parsley
1/2 cup (2 ounces) grated
  Parmesan cheese

2 ounces Gruyère cheese, grated
1/2 cup dry red wine
1/2 cup fresh bread crumbs
salt and freshly ground pepper
  to taste
1/4 cup dry red wine
1/4 cup water

Sauté the onion in the olive oil in a skillet until light golden. Add the mushroom stems and parsley and simmer for 5 minutes, stirring occasionally. Add the Parmesan cheese, Gruyère cheese and 1/2 cup wine and simmer for 5 minutes, stirring occasionally. Add the bread crumbs and mix well. Season with salt and pepper. Remove from the heat.

Spoon the cheese mixture into the mushroom caps. Arrange the prepared mushroom caps in a 9×13-inch baking dish. Pour 1/4 cup wine and the water in the bottom of the dish. Bake at 350 degrees for 40 to 45 minutes or until the tops are brown. Serve hot or cold with cocktails.

 **Chef's Tip:** The mushrooms may be prepared up to four hours in advance. Store, covered, in the refrigerator until ready to bake. To reduce watery eyes associated with chopping onions, pour a little lemon juice on your cutting board before chopping the onions.

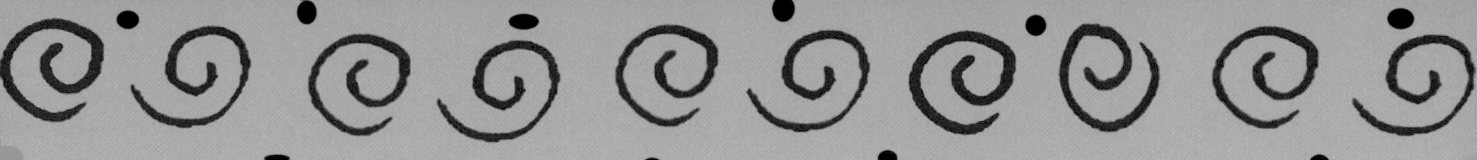

Peppers Provençal

Serves 8 to 10

1/4 cup olive oil
2 tablespoons butter
2 cups thinly sliced yellow onions
2 red bell peppers, thinly sliced

salt and pepper to taste
2 garlic cloves, minced
1/2 cup finely chopped fresh basil
1/2 teaspoon herbes de Provence

Heat the olive oil and butter in a large skillet over medium heat. Add the onions and bell peppers and toss to coat. Season with salt and pepper. Lower the heat and simmer for 45 minutes or until light brown and glazed, stirring frequently. Add the garlic, basil and herbes de Provence and cook for 5 minutes, stirring occasionally. Remove from the heat and drain. Let stand until cool. Serve at room temperature with toasted French bread.

Festive Brie

Serves 16 to 20

1 small onion, finely chopped
2 tablespoons olive oil
2 tablespoons brown sugar
1 tablespoon balsamic vinegar

6 ounces dried sweetened cranberries
2 (8-ounce) rounds Brie cheese
1/2 cup dry-roasted pistachios

Cook the onion in the olive oil in a small saucepan over medium heat until light brown, stirring occasionally. Add the brown sugar, balsamic vinegar and cranberries and cook until heated through. Place the cheese on a greased baking sheet. Bake at 350 degrees for 4 to 5 minutes or until slightly softened. Remove the cheese to a serving dish. Top with the cranberry mixture. Sprinkle with the pistachios. Serve with assorted water crackers.

Hint: An alternative to greasing the baking sheet is using parchment paper—it works far better and makes cleanup a breeze.

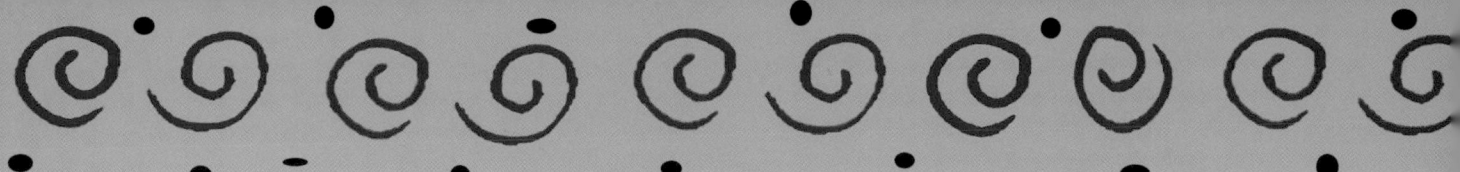

Caviar Pie

Serves 10 to 12

2 (2-ounce) jars black or red caviar
16 ounces cream cheese, softened
1 tablespoon sour cream
5 hard-cooked eggs
1 heaping tablespoon mayonnaise
1 red onion, finely chopped

To hard-cook an egg and avoid greenish-tinted yolks and shells that are tough to remove, place room-temperature eggs in a pan filled with cool tap water. Bring the water to a rolling boil, cover, remove from the heat, and let stand for 10 minutes. Place the eggs in cold water and let stand until cool to the touch. The shells should be easy to peel!

Spray a 9-inch aluminum pie plate lightly with oil. Line with plastic wrap. Strain and rinse the caviar. Drain the caviar by placing in a paper towel-lined strainer. Combine the cream cheese and sour cream in a mixing bowl and beat until blended. Spread the mixture evenly in the prepared pie plate.

Combine the eggs and mayonnaise in a food processor and process until the mixture holds together. Spread the egg mixture over the cream cheese layer. Top with the onion. Smooth with a spatula until even. Invert onto a glass serving plate. Remove the plastic wrap. Spoon the caviar over the top. Garnish with parsley and serve with water crackers.

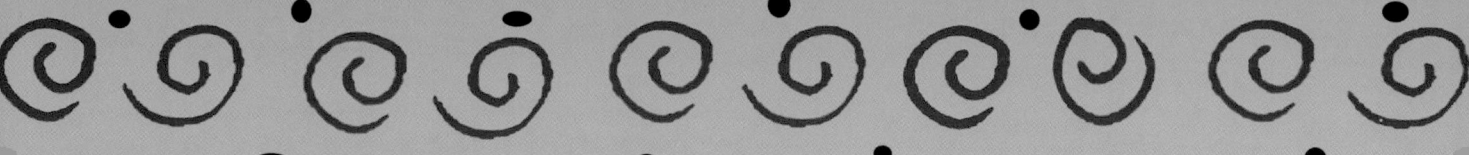

Black Olive Tapenade

Makes about 4 cups

4 to 6 garlic cloves
4 (2-ounce) cans jumbo black olives, drained

3/4 cup fresh cilantro
1/4 cup olive oil
juice of 1/2 lemon

Process the garlic in a food processor until finely chopped. Add the olives, cilantro, olive oil and lemon juice and pulse until finely chopped. Serve with crackers or sliced French bread.

Chef's Tip: For a more flavorful dish, add extra garlic and use pitted and sliced Kalamata olives instead of the canned California variety.

Hot Ham Spread with Savory Pecans

Serves 8 to 10

16 ounces cream cheese, softened
1 cup sour cream
9 ouncees thinly sliced ham, chopped
2 tablespoons dried minced onion

1 1/2 teaspoons garlic salt
1 cup chopped pecans
butter

Combine the cream cheese, sour cream, ham, onion and garlic salt in a bowl and mix well. Spoon into a 1 1/2-quart baking dish. Bake at 350 degrees for 20 minutes.
   Sauté the pecans in butter in a small sauté pan until golden brown. Sprinkle the pecans over the prepared ham mixture. Serve warm with crackers.

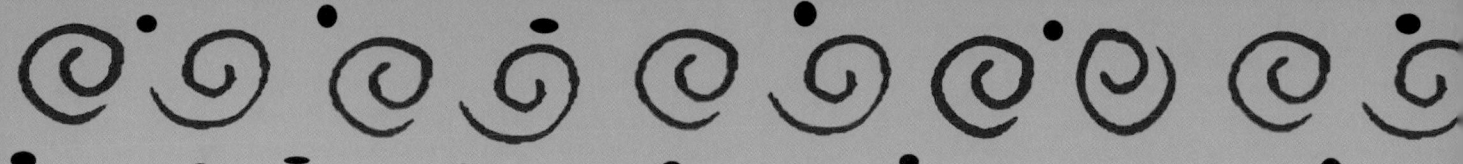

Smoked Fish Spread

Serves 15 to 20

Anchovy Aïoli

*Drain and chop
1 (2-ounce) can
anchovy fillets.
Combine with
2 cups mayonnaise,
1 minced garlic clove,
2 finely chopped
hard-cooked egg
yolks, 1/4 cup minced
parsley and
1 1/2 tablespoons
minced capers in a
bowl and mix well.
Chill, covered, for
4 hours. Serve with
assorted breads.
Makes 2 cups.*

3 cups smoked white fish,
   such as mullet, skinned,
   boned and flaked
1/2 cup finely chopped celery
1/2 cup finely chopped
   green onion
1/3 cup finely chopped green
   bell pepper
1/3 cup finely chopped red
   bell pepper

1 cup mayonnaise
2 tablespoons soy sauce
2 tablespoons Worcestershire
   sauce
1/2 teaspoon garlic powder
1/2 teaspoon hot sauce
2 to 3 tablespoons
   mayonnaise

Combine the mullet, celery, green onion, green bell pepper, red
bell pepper, 1 cup mayonnaise, soy sauce, Worcestershire sauce,
garlic powder and hot sauce in a bowl and mix well. Chill, covered,
for 8 hours. To serve, adjust the seasonings to taste and add 2 to
3 tablespoons of mayonnaise to reach the desired consistency.
Serve with crackers.

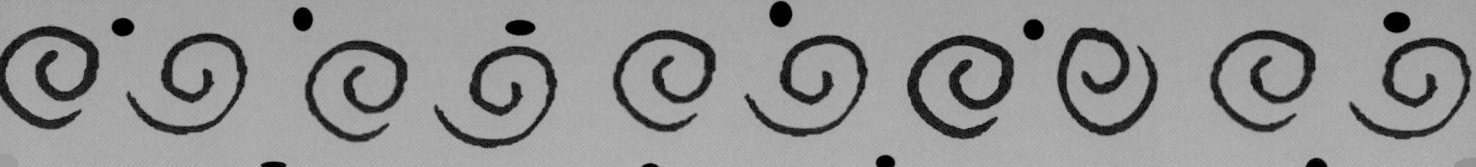

Sun-Dried Tomato and Pesto Spread

Serves 8 to 10

1½ cups boiling water
1 cup sun-dried tomatoes
8 ounces cream cheese, softened

¼ cup finely chopped onion
8 ounces basil pesto

Line a bowl with plastic wrap. Combine the water and sun-dried tomatoes in a small bowl and let stand for 3 minutes; drain. Slice the tomatoes lengthwise. Combine the cream cheese and onion in a small bowl and mix well. Layer the cream cheese mixture, sun-dried tomatoes and pesto ⅓ at a time in the prepared bowl. Cover tightly with plastic wrap. Chill in the refrigerator for 8 hours. Unwrap and invert onto a serving platter. Remove the plastic wrap. Serve with crackers.

Fresh Three-Pepper Salsa

Serves 10 to 12

6 to 8 firm ripe tomatoes, cut into
  ½-inch pieces
2 ears of corn, cooked
1 sweet onion, cut into ½-inch pieces
1 red onion, cut into ½-inch pieces
1 bunch green onions, cut into
  ½-inch pieces
2 to 3 red and/or yellow bell peppers,
  cut into ½-inch pieces
1 habanero chile, minced

6 serrano chiles, thinly sliced
2 jalapeño chiles, sliced
1 garlic clove, minced
1 bunch cilantro, chopped
2 cups cooked black beans
juice of 1 lime
¼ cup packed brown sugar
2 teaspoons salt
pepper to taste

Place the tomatoes in a colander to drain. Cut the corn kernels from the cobs into a large bowl. Combine with the onions, green onions, bell peppers, habanero chile, serrano chiles, jalapeño chiles, garlic, cilantro, black beans, lime juice, brown sugar, salt and pepper and toss gently. Add the tomatoes and toss gently to combine.

Hint: Habanero chiles are one of the hottest in existence, so be sure to use gloves when working with them. Slice and remove the seeds and ribs before mincing to protect yourself from the dangerous juices.

Santorini Salsa

Serves 12 to 15

This will transport you to the celebrated Greek Islands of Mykonos and Santorini.

4 ounces feta cheese, crumbled
1 (28-ounce) can diced tomatoes, drained
1 (4-ounce) can sliced black olives, drained
1 (4-ounce) can chopped green chiles
3 or 4 green onions, chopped
2 tablespoons chopped fresh cilantro (optional)
$1/2$ cup your favorite Italian salad dressing
salt and pepper to taste
1 (6-count) package pita bread

Combine the cheese, tomatoes, olives, green chiles, green onions, cilantro, salad dressing, salt and pepper in a large bowl and toss gently to mix. Chill, covered, to allow the flavors to blend.

Spray a skillet with cooking spray and heat to medium. Add 1 pita and cook until warm and brown on both sides, turning once. Repeat with the remaining pita bread. Cut each pita into 4 wedges. Serve the salsa with the pita bread or as an accompaniment to fish. You may substitute $1^{1/2}$ pounds chopped fresh tomatoes and 3 fresh green chiles, chopped, for the canned tomatoes and green chiles if preferred.

An unlikely blend of two cultures makes Tarpon Springs both Pinellas County's oldest city and the "Sponge Capital of the World." Its waterfront is a working seaport and shopping district with the unmistakable feel of a Grecian fishing village.

Chunky Avocado Dip

Serves 6 to 8

5 avocados, chopped
1 onion, chopped
1 tomato, peeled and
  chopped
1/4 cup fresh lemon juice
1 1/2 teaspoons garlic salt
1 teaspoon pepper

7 heaping tablespoons
  mayonnaise
1 teaspoon Worcestershire
  sauce
1 teaspoon Tabasco sauce,
  or to taste

Combine the avocados, onion, tomato, lemon juice, garlic salt and pepper in a large bowl and stir gently to mix. Add the mayonnaise, Worcestershire sauce and Tabasco sauce and mix gently. Place 3 avocado seeds in the mixture to prevent it from turning brown. Chill, covered, for up to 48 hours. Remove the avocado seeds and serve with tortilla chips.

Hint: To peel a tomato, bring a pot of water to a boil. Cut an "x" in the bottom of the tomato, just piercing the skin. Place the tomato in the boiling water for 1 minute. Allow to cool completely and then remove the peel.

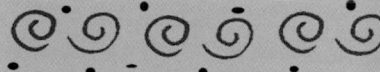

The Dunedin Fine Art Center and the David L. Mason Children's Art Museum include a unique children's art museum in addition to works of many Florida and local artists. The Junior League uses the center to host the Art Harvest Festival in Highlander Park, Dunedin.

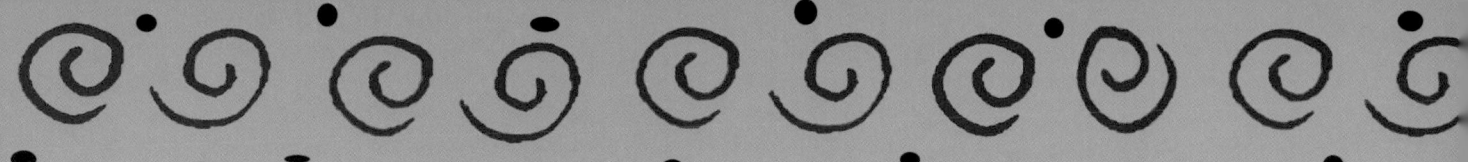

Holy Guacamole!

Serves 10

6 ripe avocados
2 tomatoes, chopped
1/4 cup minced onion
1/2 cup mayonnaise
3 tablespoons lemon juice
1/2 teaspoon Tabasco sauce
2 teaspoons chili powder
1 teaspoon garlic powder
3/4 tablespoon salt

Mash the avocados in a medium bowl. Add the tomatoes, onion, mayonnaise, lemon juice, Tabasco sauce, chili powder, garlic powder and salt and mix well. Serve with tortilla chips.

Chef's Tip: Seed the tomatoes prior to chopping to reduce the water content of the guacamole. To save half an avocado for later use, leave the seed in and cover tightly with plastic wrap before placing in the refrigerator. This will help eliminate discoloration.

Pita Chips

Try any of the dips or salsas with these easy-to-make pita chips. Separate the two halves of each small pita bread and cut each half into eight wedges. Spray the pita wedges with cooking spray, lightly season with salt, and bake at 350 degrees until light brown and crisp.

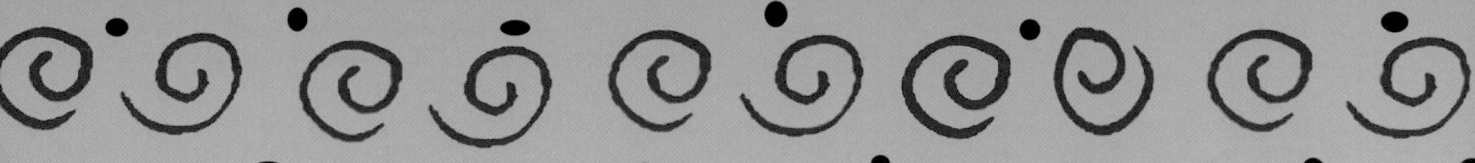

Mediterranean Dip

Serves 6 to 8

1 (7-ounce) container your favorite
  flavor hummus
1/2 cup sour cream
1 (6-ounce) jar marinated artichokes

3/4 cup shredded carrots
1/2 cup sliced black olives
4 ounces feta cheese, crumbled
1/4 cup chopped green onions

Combine the hummus and sour cream in a small bowl and mix well. Spread
evenly over a large plate. Drain and chop the artichokes and reserve the liquid.
Layer the carrots, olives, cheese, artichokes and green onions over the prepared
layer. Drizzle with a small amount of the reserved liquid. Serve with bagel chips,
pita chips or crackers.

Vidalia Onion Cheese Dip

Serves 25

3 large Vidalia onions, coarsely
  chopped
2 tablespoons margarine or butter
8 ounces sharp Cheddar cheese,
  shredded

1 cup mayonnaise
1/2 teaspoon Tabasco sauce
1 garlic clove, minced

Sauté the onions in the margarine until softened. Combine the cheese, mayonnaise,
Tabasco sauce and garlic in a medium bowl and mix well. Add the onions and mix
well. Spread the mixture in an 8×8-inch buttered baking dish. Bake at 375 degrees
for 25 minutes or until bubbly. Serve hot with tortilla chips or wheat stone crackers.

Hint: To reduce sticking when grating cheese, use a box grater sprayed with
cooking spray inside and out.

Fresh Greens with Spicy Sweet Pecans and Poppy Seed Dressing

Serves 6

Best-Ever Blue Cheese Dressing

Combine 16 ounces sour cream, 1/4 cup olive oil, 1 teaspoon Dijon mustard, 1 1/2 cups mayonnaise, 1 teaspoon yellow mustard, 1 teaspoon Worcestershire sauce and 1/4 cup lemon juice in a bowl and whisk until smooth. Whisk in 4 minced garlic cloves and 8 to 12 ounces Roquefort cheese or blue cheese. Season with salt to taste. Chill, covered, in the refrigerator. You may serve this within 30 minutes, but the flavor improves if it is chilled for 24 hours.

Spicy Sweet Pecans

1 tablespoon Creole seasoning
3 tablespoons sugar
1 1/2 cups pecans
1 tablespoon vegetable oil

Poppy Seed Dressing

1/4 cup honey
3 tablespoons cider vinegar
1 small shallot, minced
1 teaspoon poppy seeds
salt and pepper to taste

Salad

4 cups field greens
1 tomato, seeded and chopped
1/2 cup each chopped red and yellow bell pepper
1/2 cup sliced cucumber
1 medium carrot, sliced
2 green onions, sliced
1/2 cup craisins
3/4 cup sliced strawberries
5 ounces feta cheese, crumbled

For the pecans, mix the Creole seasoning and sugar in a sealable plastic bag. Toss the pecans with the oil in a bowl. Add to the seasoning mixture and mix to coat well. Spread in a single layer on a baking sheet. Bake at 350 degrees for 10 to 15 minutes or until golden brown, checking frequently to prevent overbrowning. Cool to room temperature.

For the dressing, combine the honey and vinegar in a bowl and whisk to mix well. Whisk in the shallot and poppy seeds and season with salt and pepper.

For the salad, combine the field greens with the tomato, bell peppers, cucumber, carrot and green onions in a large salad bowl. Add the craisins, strawberries and cheese and toss to mix well. Sprinkle with the pecans and serve with the dressing.

Hint: Prepare extra pecans and serve them with Sugared Cranberries (page 91) as a snack or appetizer at your next party.

Fresh Pear Salad

Serves 8

Dijon Vinaigrette
1/2 cup olive oil
1 cup rice vinegar
splash of balsamic vinegar
1 tablespoon Dijon mustard
1 tablespoon sugar
1 tablespoon seasoned salt

Salad
8 cups mixed salad greens
1 or 2 red or green pears, thinly sliced
3/4 cup sweetened dried cranberries
  or golden raisins
1/2 cup (2 ounces) crumbled blue
  cheese
1 cup chopped walnuts

For the vinaigrette, combine the olive oil, rice vinegar and balsamic vinegar in a jar or cruet. Add the mustard, sugar and seasoned salt and shake to mix well.

For the salad, combine the salad greens, pears, dried cranberries, cheese and walnuts in a salad bowl. Add the dressing and toss to mix well.

Spinach and Avocado Salad with Toasted Walnuts

Serves 6

Sweet and Sour Dressing
1/4 cup cider vinegar
1/4 cup vegetable oil
1/4 cup sugar
1/4 teaspoon garlic salt
1/4 teaspoon celery salt

Salad
1 package fresh spinach
1 avocado, chopped
1 Granny Smith apple, chopped
  (optional)
1/2 cup toasted chopped walnuts

For the dressing, combine the vinegar, oil, sugar, garlic salt and celery salt in a bowl and whisk until smooth. Store in the refrigerator for up to 24 hours.

For the salad, combine the spinach with the avocado, apple and walnuts in a large salad bowl. Shake the dressing and add to the salad; toss to coat well.

Hint: To toast walnuts, place them on a baking sheet and toast at 350 degrees for 5 minutes. Shake the baking sheet and toast for several minutes longer or until light brown.

Spinach Salad with Hot Citrus Dressing

Serves 8

Salad

2 pounds baby spinach leaves
4 oranges, separated into sections, or 2 (11-ounce) cans mandarin oranges, drained
1 large purple onion, thinly sliced
4 ounces goat cheese, crumbled
1 cup dried cherries
1/2 cup toasted pecans, chopped

Hot Citrus Dressing

1 (6-ounce) can frozen orange juice concentrate, thawed
1/3 cup red wine vinegar
1 teaspoon hot sauce
1 cup packed light brown sugar
1 tablespoon grated orange zest
1 teaspoon dry mustard
1 teaspoon salt
1 cup peanut oil

For the salad, line 8 salad plates with the spinach and arrange the orange sections and onion slices over the spinach. Top with the cheese, dried cherries and pecans.

For the dressing, combine the orange juice concentrate, vinegar, hot sauce, brown sugar, orange zest, dry mustard and salt in a blender and process to blend well. Add the peanut oil gradually, processing constantly until smooth. Pour into a saucepan and bring to a boil. Reduce the heat and simmer for 10 minutes. Drizzle over the salad and serve immediately.

Hint: This dressing makes more than enough for the salad; store the remaining dressing in the refrigerator and reheat in the microwave to serve.

Spinach Salad with Creamy Garlic Dressing

Serves 6 to 8

Creamy Garlic Dressing
3/4 cup vegetable oil
6 tablespoons red wine
  vinegar
1/4 cup sour cream
2 tablespoons sugar
2 garlic cloves, pressed
2 teaspoons chopped
  fresh parsley
1 teaspoon dry mustard
1 teaspoon salt
pepper to taste

Salad
1 (10-ounce) package fresh
  baby spinach
1 1/2 cups sliced mushrooms
1 bunch green onions, sliced
1 tomato, sliced
4 slices bacon, crisp-fried and
  crumbled

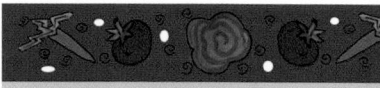

The Scot Shop in Dunedin has been a staple for our community since 1960—providing used clothes and housewares at discounted prices. The Junior League of Clearwater-Dunedin uses the shop as its main source of income.

For the dressing, combine the oil, vinegar, sour cream, sugar, garlic, parsley, dry mustard, salt and pepper in a cruet or jar and mix well. Chill in the refrigerator for 24 hours.

For the salad, combine the spinach, mushrooms, green onions, tomato and bacon in a large salad bowl. Shake the dressing and add to the salad; toss to coat well.

Bacon and Blue Cheese Salad with Easy Caesar Dressing

Serves 6

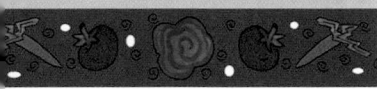

Homemade Garlic Croutons

Cut 4 slices French bread into 3/4-inch cubes. Combine 2 tablespoons butter, 1/4 cup olive oil and 2 minced large garlic cloves in a sauté pan over medium heat; sauté until the garlic is fragrant. Add the bread cubes and toss to coat well. Sauté until the croutons are light brown.

Easy Caesar Dressing
1/2 cup olive oil
1/4 cup fresh lemon juice
1 teaspoon Worcestershire sauce
2 garlic cloves, minced
1/2 cup (2 ounces) freshly grated Parmesan cheese
salt and pepper to taste

Salad
1 large head romaine lettuce, or 3 romaine lettuce hearts, torn
6 slices bacon, crisp-fried and crumbled
1/2 cup (2 ounces) crumbled blue cheese
1 cup Homemade Garlic Croutons (at left)

For the dressing, combine the olive oil, lemon juice, Worcestershire sauce, garlic and Parmesan cheese in a blender or food processor and process until smooth. Season with salt and pepper. Store in the refrigerator for up to 2 days.

For the salad, combine the romaine lettuce with the bacon and cheese in a large bowl. Add the dressing and toss to coat well. Top with Homemade Garlic Croutons.

Pappas' Riverside Greek Salad

Serves 4 or more

Pappas' Riverside Greek Salad is legendary throughout the southern United States.

Potato Salad

6 boiling potatoes with skins
2 white onions, thinly sliced
1/2 cup thinly sliced green onions
1/2 small green bell pepper, thinly sliced
1/4 cup chopped parsley
1/2 cup mayonnaise
white vinegar to taste
salt to taste

Greek Salad

1 large head lettuce
12 leaves spinach or watercress
2 tomatoes, each cut into 6 wedges
1 cucumber, peeled and
   cut lengthwise into 8 strips

1 avocado, cut into wedges
8 ounces feta cheese
1 green bell pepper, cut into 8 rings
4 beet slices
4 peeled cooked shrimp
4 anchovy fillets
12 black Greek olives
12 medium-hot Salonika peppers
4 radishes, cut into flowers
4 whole green onions
1/4 cup olive oil
1/4 cup vegetable oil
1/2 cup white vinegar
oregano to taste

For the potato salad, combine the potatoes with enough water to cover in a saucepan and cook for 30 minutes or until tender but not mushy. Drain the potatoes, cool slightly and peel. Slice into a bowl and add the onions, green onions, bell pepper and parsley. Add the mayonnaise and vinegar and mix lightly. Season with salt.

For the Greek salad, line a large platter with lettuce leaves. Shred the remaining lettuce. Place 3 cups of the potato salad in a mound in the center of the platter and sprinkle with the shredded lettuce. Top with the spinach and some of the tomato wedges. Arrange the remaining tomato wedges around the potatoes and place the cucumber strips between the wedges. Add the avocado. Arrange the cheese, bell pepper rings, and beet slices over the salad. Top each beet with a shrimp and anchovy fillet. Add the olives, Salonika peppers, radishes and green onions. Blend the olive oil and vegetable oil in a small bowl. Sprinkle the salad with the vinegar, the oil mixture and oregano. Serve immediately.

Ceviche Salad

Serves 6

Indian Rocks Beach is home to Keegan's Seafood Grill, where they have adapted this seafood salad from Central and South America. It is at its best two full days after being prepared.

Ceviche

Archaeological evidence suggests that the Inca rulers made the mountain site of Machu Picchu their retreat estate. In order to have fresh seafood daily, a system of roads was established, and runners were able to bring seafood from the coast in a steady supply. Somewhere in the process, citrus juice was used to ensure freshness, and ceviche was created. Ceviche has evolved since to include any white fish, shellfish, vegetables, and citrus.

Marinated Seafood

12 ounces grouper, cut into bite-size pieces
12 ounces scallops and/or shrimp
4 ounces onion, very thinly sliced into 1-inch pieces
4 ounces white cabbage, very thinly sliced into 1-inch pieces
2 ribs celery heart, very thinly sliced
3/4 cup freshly squeezed lemon juice
1/2 cup freshly squeezed lime juice
salt and pepper to taste

Salad

1/3 cup corn
1 cup chopped tomato
1 teaspoon minced garlic
1 tablespoon chopped jalapeño chile
1/3 bunch cilantro, chopped
rice wine vinegar or other vinegar to taste
1/4 cup olive oil

To marinate the seafood, combine the grouper and scallops with the onion, cabbage and celery in a bowl. Add the lemon juice and lime juice and season with salt and pepper. Marinate in the refrigerator for 24 hours or longer to "cook."

For the salad, add the corn, tomato, garlic, jalapeño chile and cilantro to the marinated seafood and mix well. Add vinegar and the olive oil and adjust the seasonings; mix gently.

Macadamia Lobster Over Summer Greens

Serves 4

Alfano's Restaurant, a landmark in Belleair, has generously shared this summer lobster salad recipe.

Sesame Vinaigrette
2 tablespoons sesame oil
2 tablespoons vegetable oil
2 tablespoons honey
2 tablespoons dark soy sauce
1/2 cup rice wine vinegar

Salad
4 (4-ounce) cold-water
   lobster tails
2 eggs, beaten
1 cup crushed macadamias
8 cups torn baby lettuces
2/3 cup crumbled Gorgonzola
   cheese
2/3 cup sun-dried cranberries

For the vinaigrette, combine the sesame oil and vegetable oil in a bowl and whisk until smooth. Whisk in the honey and soy sauce. Add the vinegar gradually, whisking constantly until smooth.

For the salad, split the lobsters along the back and pull the meat up and over the shell, leaving it connected at the base. Flatten the lobster meat lightly with a mallet, taking care not to detach it from the shell. Dip into the beaten eggs and coat with the macadamias, pressing the nuts onto the top and sides of the lobster; arrange the meat on top of the shell. Place on a baking sheet and bake at 350 degrees for 20 to 25 minutes or until cooked through.

Toss the lettuces with the vinaigrette in a bowl. Spoon onto salad plates and top with the cheese and cranberries. Place a lobster tail on each salad and garnish with edible flowers.

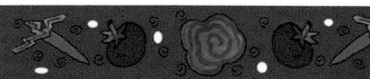

The Jolly Trolley

The Jolly Trolley, a San Francisco-style trolley car, travels throughout Clearwater Beach and to downtown, taking residents and tourists to the many restaurants and attractions in both areas.

Asian Steak Salad with Spicy Honey-Basil Marinade

Serves 6

Spicy Honey-Basil Marinade
2 ginseng tea bags or green tea bags
1 cup boiling water
1 tablespoon honey
2 tablespoons fresh lemon juice
2 teaspoons olive oil
2 tablespoons pine nuts
1/2 cup packed basil leaves
2 garlic cloves, minced
1 jalapeño chile
1/4 teaspoon salt
1/4 teaspoon white pepper or
   black pepper

Asian Dressing
3 tablespoons olive oil
2 tablespoons fresh lemon juice
1 tablespoon Dijon mustard
1 teaspoon freshly grated gingerroot
1 to 2 garlic cloves, minced
salt and pepper to taste

Salad
1 pound flank steak
1 medium head romaine lettuce, torn
1 medium head red leaf lettuce, torn
1 cucumber, cut into halves
   lengthwise and sliced
1 tomato or plum tomato, thinly sliced
1/2 cup (2 ounces) grated Parmesan
   cheese

For the marinade, steep the tea bags in the boiling water for 5 minutes. Combine the tea and the contents of the tea bags with the honey, lemon juice and olive oil in a blender. Add the pine nuts, basil, garlic, jalapeño chile, salt and white pepper and process until smooth. This may be stored in the refrigerator for up to 1 week.

For the dressing, combine the olive oil, lemon juice, mustard, gingerroot, garlic, salt and pepper in a bowl and mix well. Store in the refrigerator.

For the salad, marinate the steak in the Honey-Basil Marinade in a bowl for 30 minutes; drain. Grill the steak until done to taste. Let stand for 5 minutes and cut diagonally across the grain into thin slices.

Combine the romaine lettuce, red leaf lettuce, cucumber and tomato in a salad bowl. Add the dressing and toss to mix well. Spoon onto plates and arrange the steak over the top; sprinkle with the Parmesan cheese.

Grilled Chicken Salad

Serves 6

3 pounds boneless skinless
  chicken breasts
1 (12-ounce) bottle Italian
  salad dressing
2 teaspoons Italian seasoning
1/2 cup raisins
2 cups chopped celery
1 tablespoon parsley flakes

1 1/2 tablespoons garlic
  powder
salt and pepper to taste
1 cup ranch salad dressing
1 cup mayonnaise
salad greens
chopped almonds
chopped scallions

Combine the chicken with the Italian salad dressing and Italian seasoning in a bowl. Marinate in the refrigerator for 8 hours or longer. Grill until cooked through, taking care not to overcook. Cut into bite-size pieces.

Combine the raisins and celery with the chicken in a bowl. Add the parsley flakes, garlic powder, salt and pepper and mix well. Add the ranch salad dressing and mayonnaise and stir gently. Chill until serving time.

Add additional ranch salad dressing and mayonnaise if necessary at serving time and mix well. Serve over salad greens and sprinkle with chopped almonds and scallions.

You may also serve the chicken salad in warmed croissants.

 **Heart-Healthy Tip:** Choose from vegetable oil and margarine with no more than 2 grams of saturated fatty acids per tablespoon—canola, corn, olive, safflower, sesame, soybean, sunflower, or walnut. Select those that contain liquid vegetable oil as the first ingredient.

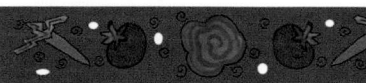

Classic Vinaigrette

Combine 1 tablespoon olive oil, 1 tablespoon vinegar or lemon juice, 1/4 teaspoon dry mustard, 1/4 teaspoon salt and 1/4 teaspoon pepper in a bowl and whisk until smooth. Whisk in 2 additional tablespoons olive oil. Add 1 additional tablespoon vinegar or lemon juice, 3 additional tablespoons olive oil and 1 minced garlic clove; mix well. Store in a covered jar in the refrigerator. Shake well before using.

Thai Chicken Salad

Serves 6 to 8

Peanut Dressing
1/4 cup reduced-sodium soy sauce
2 tablespoons sesame oil
2 tablespoons rice vinegar
1/4 cup peanut butter
2 tablespoons brown sugar
1 garlic clove, crushed
2 tablespoons garlic chile paste
1 teaspoon ground ginger or grated
    gingerroot
1/2 cup Italian salad dressing
1/4 cup orange juice

Salad
3 pounds deli roasted chicken
4 to 6 cups shredded lettuce
1 cup shredded carrots
1 cup sliced pea pods
julienned red and/or green bell
    peppers
8 green onions, sliced
1/2 cup chopped parsley
1 (3-ounce) can crisp rice noodles
1/2 cup dry-roasted peanuts

For the dressing, combine the soy sauce, sesame oil and vinegar in a bowl and whisk until smooth. Whisk in the peanut butter, brown sugar, garlic, chile paste and ginger. Add the Italian salad dressing and orange juice and mix well.

For the salad, shred the chicken into bite-size pieces. Combine with the lettuce, carrots, pea pods, bell peppers, green onions and parsley in a bowl. Add half the dressing and toss to mix well. Spoon onto a serving platter and sprinkle the noodles around the edge. Sprinkle the peanuts over the top and serve with the remaining dressing.

Heart-Healthy Tip: Make your own reduced-sodium soy sauce by diluting regular soy sauce with an equal amount of water.

The Columbia's 1905 Salad

Serves 4

Most people can't resist the 1905 Salad served at the Columbia Restaurant.

The Columbia's 1905 Dressing

4 garlic cloves, minced
1 teaspoon Worcestershire sauce
1 teaspoon oregano
1/2 cup extra-virgin Spanish olive oil or Italian olive oil
2 tablespoons white wine vinegar
2 teaspoons lemon juice
salt and pepper to taste

Salad

1/2 head iceberg lettuce
2 ripe tomatoes, each cut into 8 wedges
1/2 cup (2 ounces) julienned Swiss cheese
1/2 cup julienned ham, turkey or shrimp
1/4 cup pitted green Spanish olives
2 teaspoons grated Romano cheese

For the dressing, combine the garlic, Worcestershire sauce and oregano in a bowl and whisk until smooth. Whisk in the olive oil gradually. Stir in the vinegar and lemon juice and season with salt and pepper.

For the salad, combine the lettuce, tomatoes, Swiss cheese, ham and olives in a salad bowl. Add the dressing and toss to coat well. Add the Romano cheese and toss again.

Sangria

Sangria is a popular beachside drink in the area—compliments of the Columbia Restaurant. Originally built in Ybor City in 1905 by the Gonzmart family, the Columbia now has six locations throughout the state, including one on Sand Key at Clearwater Beach. The Columbia's famous sangria and paella give diners a feel of Spain in our local community.

Curried Apple Soup

Serves 5

3 tablespoons butter
2 onions, chopped
3 ribs celery, chopped
3 tablespoons flour
2 teaspoons curry powder
1/2 teaspoon freshly
   ground pepper
4 cups chicken stock and/or
   vegetable stock

2 tart medium apples, peeled
   and chopped
1/2 cup light cream
1 teaspoon lemon juice
1 tablespoon Calvados or
   brandy (optional)
salt to taste

Built in 1897, Clearwater's community Royalty Theatre is the oldest theater in the state. In addition to showcasing a wide variety of performances, it houses historic exhibits on Florida, musical instruments, and the classical arts.

Combine the butter, onions and celery in a microwave-safe 8-cup dish. Microwave on High for 5 to 6 minutes or until the vegetables are tender-crisp, stirring halfway through the cooking process. Stir in the flour, curry powder and pepper. Microwave on High for 1 minute. Stir in the chicken stock. Microwave, covered, on High for 10 to 12 minutes or until slightly thickened.

Add the apples. Microwave, covered, on High for 10 to 12 minutes or until the apples are tender. Stir in the cream and lemon juice. Microwave, covered, on Medium for 5 to 6 minutes or until heated through. Stir in the Calvados and let stand for 5 minutes. Season with salt and ladle into soup bowls.

Carrot Ginger Soup

Serves 6

2 tablespoons unsalted butter
1 white onion, chopped
3 large carrots, peeled and sliced
1½ ribs celery, chopped
2 large garlic cloves, chopped
1 (1-inch) piece gingerroot, peeled and finely grated
4 cups chicken stock or chicken broth

½ cup heavy cream (optional)
5 sprigs cilantro, chopped
kosher salt or sea salt and freshly ground pepper to taste
2 tablespoons minced scallions
3 tablespoons sour cream or yogurt (optional)

Melt the butter in a large saucepan over medium heat. Add the onion, carrots, celery, garlic and gingerroot. Sauté until the vegetables begin to caramelize. Add the chicken stock and simmer for 45 minutes or until the carrots are tender.

Process the mixture in a blender or food processor until smooth. Strain the mixture into a clean saucepan. Add the cream, cilantro, kosher salt and pepper and bring to a simmer. Remove from the heat and ladle into soup bowls. Top with the scallions and sour cream.

Chef's Tip: This soup is delicious served hot or cold, with or without the cream. You may need to adjust the seasonings if it is served cold.

Hearty Fish Chowder

Serves 6

1 (14-ounce) can tomatoes
1 (8-ounce) can tomato sauce
1½ cups dry white wine
¼ cup olive oil
1 cup chopped onion
1 cup chopped green bell
  pepper
4 garlic cloves, crushed
2 bay leaves
¼ teaspoon thyme
¼ teaspoon marjoram
1 teaspoon salt

1 pound red snapper, cut into
  1-inch pieces
8 ounces shrimp, peeled
8 ounces scallops
1 (10-ounce) can baby clams,
  drained
½ teaspoon Tabasco sauce
juice of 1 lemon
¼ teaspoon pepper
½ cup chopped parsley
½ cup chopped scallions

Combine the tomatoes, tomato sauce, wine, olive oil, onion, bell pepper, garlic, bay leaves, thyme, marjoram and salt in a large saucepan and mix well. Simmer, covered, for 2 to 2½ hours or until the desired consistency, removing the cover during the last 10 minutes of cooking time.

Add the red snapper and simmer for 5 minutes. Add the shrimp and simmer for 2 to 3 minutes or until pink. Add the scallops and simmer for 3 minutes. Stir in the clams, Tabasco sauce, lemon juice and pepper. Discard the bay leaves and ladle into soup bowls. Sprinkle with parsley and scallions. You may also garnish with mussels if desired and serve with French bread and a salad.

Chef's Tip: Try substituting flounder, crab meat, mahi mahi, or tilapia to find your favorite flavor.

The Belleview Biltmore Resort and Spa in Belleair was built in 1897 and is the oldest occupied wooden building still used for its original purpose. Tours highlight not only the historic architecture, but also rumors of the ghosts that haunt the resort, the underground railway, and hidden passageways.

Clams di Zuppa

Serves 4 to 6

36 cherrystone clams
2 garlic cloves, minced
1 cup chopped onion
2 tablespoons olive oil
2 (28-ounce) cans peeled tomatoes, crushed

1/2 cup dry white wine
2 tablespoons chopped parsley
1 teaspoon oregano
1/2 teaspoon dried basil leaves
1/4 teaspoon salt
1/2 teaspoon crushed red pepper

Scrub the clams and rinse about 6 times to remove the sand. Combine with 2 inches of water in a large saucepan. Steam, covered, until the clams open, discarding any clams that do not open. Drain, reserving the broth. Strain the broth and reserve 3 cups.

Sauté the garlic and onion in the olive oil in a saucepan until transparent. Add the tomatoes, wine, parsley, oregano, basil, salt and red pepper and mix well. Simmer for 20 minutes. Stir in the reserved clam broth. Simmer until heated through. Add the clams and mix gently. Simmer until heated through. Ladle into soup bowls and serve with crusty Italian bread or French bread.

This will serve 6 to 8 as an appetizer.

 **Chef's Tip:** A variation for the Clams di Zuppa is to add fresh spinach just before serving; it will add both texture and taste to the soup.

Frenchy's Café Seafood Gumbo

Serves 12

Frenchy's Restaurants on Clearwater Beach are famous for grouper sandwiches and fun. They generously offered this recipe for their famed seafood gumbo to include in the book.

1/2 cup (1 stick) butter
1 onion, chopped
1 large green bell pepper, chopped
4 ribs celery, chopped
2 tablespoons chopped celery leaves
1 green onion, chopped
1 1/2 tablespoons minced garlic
1/2 cup flour
3 1/4 tablespoons gumbo filé
1 1/2 tablespoons paprika
1 bay leaf
1 1/2 teaspoons oregano
1 1/2 teaspoons basil

1 1/2 teaspoons thyme
1 1/2 teaspoons cayenne pepper
1/2 teaspoon black pepper
1/2 cup Burgundy wine
6 1/4 cups canned diced tomatoes with juice
1 1/4 cups water
1 1/2 ounces ham base
2 cups frozen okra
2 cups frozen corn
8 ounces crab meat
8 ounces (110- to 130-count) shrimp
8 ounces scallops
8 ounces grouper

Pier 60

Pier 60, Clearwater's famed 1,050-foot sightseeing and fishing pier, is the focal point of the beach—along with Pier 60 Park. Families gather at the park at dusk to celebrate beautiful sunsets overlooking the Gulf of Mexico.

Melt the butter in a large saucepan. Add the onion, bell pepper, celery, celery leaves, green onion and garlic. Sauté for 10 minutes.

Stir in the flour, gumbo filé, paprika, bay leaf, oregano, basil, thyme, cayenne pepper and black pepper. Cook for 15 minutes, stirring constantly. Stir in the wine. Add the tomatoes, water, ham base, okra and corn. Bring to a boil and reduce the heat.

Add the crab meat, shrimp, scallops and grouper. Simmer for 1 1/2 hours. Let stand for 10 minutes. Discard the bay leaf and ladle into soup bowls.

New Orleans-Style Gumbo

Serves 20

4 (10-ounce) packages frozen okra
1 pound smoked sausage, chopped
3 tablespoons vegetable oil
4 cups water
6 tablespoons vegetable oil
6 tablespoons flour
3 large onions, finely chopped
1 tablespoon garlic powder
2 tablespoons liquid crab boil
1 tablespoon thyme
7 quarts water

2 pounds shrimp, finely chopped
6 gumbo blue crabs, cleaned and
   cut into halves
1 pound crab meat, picked
8 bay leaves
1/2 cup finely chopped Italian parsley
1 (15-ounce) can tomato sauce
2 tablespoons salt
3 pounds medium shrimp
6 cups steamed rice
1/2 cup gumbo filé

Steam the okra for 12 minutes in a steamer; drain. Brown the sausage in
3 tablespoons oil in a skillet over high heat; drain. Combine the okra and sausage
in a large stockpot and cook over medium heat for 5 minutes, stirring constantly.
Add 4 cups water and simmer, covered, while preparing the roux.

Heat 6 tablespoons oil in a saucepan over low heat. Stir in the flour. Cook for
20 minutes or until a rich brown, stirring constantly and taking care not to burn.
Add the onions, garlic powder, crab boil and thyme. Cook for 5 minutes, stirring
constantly. Add to the sausage mixture in the stockpot.

Add 7 quarts water and cook over low heat for 10 minutes, stirring constantly.
Stir in the chopped shrimp, crabs, crab meat, bay leaves, parsley, tomato sauce
and salt. Simmer, covered, for 30 minutes, stirring occasionally.

Increase the heat to high and add the whole shrimp. Cook for 5 minutes
longer, stirring constantly. Remove from the heat and let stand, covered, for
15 minutes or longer; discard the bay leaves. Reheat to serve if necessary.

Spoon the rice into bowls. Ladle the gumbo over the rice and serve with
the filé to sprinkle over the top.

Chef's Tip: Be organized. Make sure all ingredients are cleaned, drained,
sliced, chopped and ready to go before you start.

Green Chile Stew

Serves 4

2 pounds pork tenderloin, cut into bite-size pieces
1 onion, chopped
1 tablespoon vegetable oil
1 tablespoon flour
3 garlic cloves, chopped
1 1/2 cups beef broth
1 (10-ounce) can diced tomatoes with green chiles
1 (4-ounce) can chopped green chiles
2 carrots, chopped
1 1/4 teaspoons cumin
salt and pepper to taste
2 potatoes, chopped

Sauté the pork and onion in the oil in a large saucepan for 5 minutes. Stir in the flour and garlic and sauté for 5 minutes or until the pork is brown. Add the beef broth, tomatoes, chiles, carrots, cumin, salt and pepper. Bring to a boil and reduce the heat. Simmer for 1 hour, stirring occasionally. Add the potatoes and simmer for 30 minutes or until the potatoes are tender, adding water or additional beef broth if needed for the desired consistency. Serve with corn bread.

Cream of Onion Soup Duchess

Serves 12

Bob Heilman's Beachcomber has been a favorite of Clearwater Beach for more than 50 years. Vintage postcards memorialize the changes over the years in this restaurant for fine dining.

3 Vidalia onions or other sweet onions, grated
1 small carrot, grated
4 cups rich chicken stock, heated
1/2 cup (1 stick) butter
1/4 cup flour
1 cup light cream, heated
salt and pepper to taste
1 bunch parsley, finely chopped
grated Parmesan cheese to taste

Combine the onions and carrot with the chicken stock in a saucepan. Cook for 10 minutes. Melt the butter in a heavy saucepan and blend in the flour. Cook until smooth. Remove from the heat and add the chicken stock and vegetables, stirring constantly to incorporate the roux. Bring to a boil and cook until thickened, stirring constantly. Stir in the cream and season with salt and pepper. Ladle into soup cups and sprinkle with the parsley and Parmesan cheese.

Red Pepper Brie Soup

Serves 4

The Westin Innisbrook Resort serves up not only delicious food but good golf as well. Innisbrook is home to the famous Copperhead Course and the annual PGA Tour.

2 tablespoons olive oil
1 rib celery, chopped
1 carrot, chopped
1/2 cup chopped onion
1 garlic clove, chopped
2 cups water
1 ounce chicken base
3 large red bell peppers, roasted
4 1/2 ounces Brie cheese, rind
  removed and chopped

4 1/2 ounces cream cheese, chopped
2 sprigs fresh basil
1 sprig fresh thyme
1/2 sprig fresh rosemary
2 bay leaves
cornstarch
1 cup heavy cream, heated
salt and pepper to taste

Heat the olive oil in a saucepan. Add the celery, carrot and onion and sauté for 5 minutes. Add the garlic and cook until the garlic is light brown. Stir in the water, chicken base, bell peppers, Brie cheese, cream cheese, basil, thyme, rosemary and bay leaves. Bring to a boil and reduce the heat. Simmer for 30 minutes.

Blend enough cornstarch to thicken the soup with a small amount of water. Add to the soup and cook until thickened, stirring constantly. Process in a blender or food processor until smooth. Strain back into the saucepan and add the heated cream. Season with salt and pepper and ladle into soup bowls.

Venetian Vegetable Soup

Serves 8 to 10

1 large rib celery
1 large tomato, cored
2 small zucchini
1 medium potato, peeled
1 medium carrot, peeled
6 asparagus spears
2 tablespoons olive oil
2 tablespoons unsalted butter
1 onion, chopped

1 small wedge green cabbage or
   Savoy cabbage, coarsely chopped
white portions of 2 leeks, thinly sliced
1 bay leaf
salt and freshly ground pepper
   to taste
2 quarts boiling water or chicken stock
1/3 cup tomato sauce

Chop the celery, tomato, zucchini, potato, carrot and asparagus into 1/4-inch pieces. Heat the olive oil with the butter in a saucepan over medium-high heat. Add the onion and reduce the heat to medium-low. Sauté for 10 to 15 minutes or until brown, stirring frequently. Add the chopped vegetables, cabbage and leeks. Stir in the bay leaf and season with salt and pepper. Sauté for 15 minutes, stirring frequently with a wooden spoon.

Add the water and tomato sauce. Bring to a boil and reduce the heat. Simmer, partially covered, for 15 minutes. Remove the bay leaf and add additional boiling water if needed for the desired consistency. Ladle into soup bowls and serve with freshly grated Parmesan cheese.

 **Heart-Healthy Tip:** The American Heart Association (AHA) recommends a balanced diet including a variety of foods low in total fat, saturated fatty acids, cholesterol, and sodium. The AHA does not recommend regularly using food substitutes or supplements to lower blood cholesterol levels.

Sherried Wild Rice Soup

Serves 8 to 10

1 cup uncooked wild rice
4 cups water
1 teaspoon salt
1 onion, chopped
1/4 cup (1/2 stick) butter
1/2 cup thinly sliced celery
2 cups sliced mushrooms
1/4 cup flour
3 to 4 (14-ounce) cans
  chicken broth or
  vegetable broth

1/2 teaspoon curry powder
1/2 teaspoon dry mustard
1/2 teaspoon chervil
1/2 teaspoon (or less) white
  pepper
2/3 cup dry sherry
2 cups half-and-half

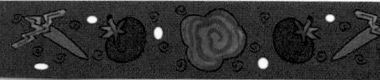

Rinse the wild rice in running water until the water runs clear. Bring the water and salt to a boil in a saucepan. Add the rice and reduce the heat. Simmer for 45 minutes or until the rice is tender; drain any excess water.

Sauté the onion in the butter in a saucepan until golden brown. Stir in the celery and mushrooms and sauté for 5 minutes. Stir in the flour. Add the chicken broth gradually and cook until slightly thickened, stirring constantly.

Add the rice, curry powder, dry mustard, chervil and white pepper. Reduce the heat and stir in the sherry and half-and-half. Heat just to the simmering point; do not boil. Add additional chicken broth if needed for the desired consistency. Ladle into soup bowls and garnish with minced parsley, chives or additional sliced mushrooms.

Clearwater Jazz Holiday, held in October each year at Coachman Park in downtown Clearwater, has brought world-class jazz musicians to the area for over 25 years. The three-day festival provides free jazz music— ranging from smooth jazz to New Orleans blues.

Beef Tenderloin with Balsamic Sauce 86

Mock Carpaccio 86

Asian Short Ribs 87

Pot Roast with Wine 87

South African Meat Loaf 88

Lamb Paillarde Burger 89

Osso Buco 90

Apricot-Glazed Pork 91

Sugared Cranberries 91

Florida Orange-Glazed Pork Chops 92

Grilled Pineapple Chicken 93

Lemon and Rosemary Chicken 93

Gasparilla Drunken Chicken with Sweet Potato Mash 94, 95

Chicken Scaloppine with Mango-Balsamic Sauce 96

Elegant Penne 97

Roasted Red Pepper Lasagna 98

Polenta and Spinach Lasagna 99

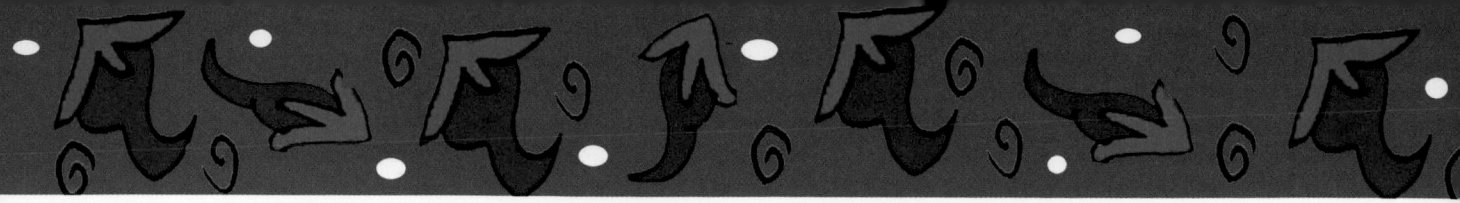

Beef Tenderloin with Balsamic Sauce Serves 4

Beef Tenderloin
2 tablespoons sea salt
1 tablespoon coarse pepper
4 (6-ounce) beef filets
   mignons
2 tablespoons olive oil

Balsamic Sauce
$1/4$ cup dry red wine
$1/4$ cup dry cooking sherry
3 tablespoons balsamic
   vinegar
1 shallot, chopped
2 garlic cloves, chopped
2 egg yolks
$1/3$ cup butter, melted

For the beef, rub the sea salt and pepper over both sides of the steaks. Heat the olive oil in an iron skillet over high heat. Add the steaks and cook for 2 to 3 minutes on each side or until brown. Place in a 350-degree oven and bake for 8 to 15 minutes or until done to taste.

For the sauce, combine the red wine, sherry, balsamic vinegar, shallot and garlic in a saucepan. Bring to a boil and cook for 2 minutes. Cool the mixture. Whisk in the egg yolks and cook over low heat for 2 to 5 minutes or until thickened, whisking constantly. Whisk in the butter. Serve over the steaks.

Hint: Serve leftover beef tenderloin for lunch the next day in a Mock Carpaccio.

Mock Carpaccio

Cut a chilled 1-pound flank steak diagonally into thin slices and arrange on a platter. Sprinkle with $1/2$ cup chopped onion, 2 tablespoons cold-pressed olive oil and 1 tablespoon drained capers. Grind fresh pepper over the top and sprinkle with salt. Shave 2 ounces pecorino Romano cheese over the top and serve as a light lunch or appetizer.

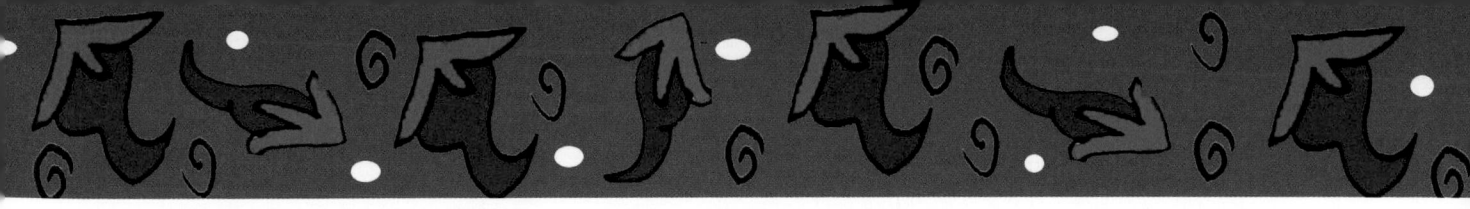

Asian Short Ribs

Serves 6 to 8

1/2 cup soy sauce
1/2 cup water
1/4 cup dark-roasted sesame oil
2 1/2 tablespoons packed brown sugar
2/3 cup sliced green onions
1 tablespoon crushed garlic

1 tablespoon grated gingerroot
1/2 teaspoon ground red garlic
1 1/2 tablespoons toasted sesame seeds
pepper to taste
4 pounds beef short ribs

Combine the soy sauce, water, sesame oil and brown sugar in a bowl and mix well. Stir in the green onions, crushed garlic, gingerroot, red garlic, sesame seeds and pepper. Combine with the short ribs in a roasting pan, turning the ribs to coat well. Roast at 325 degrees for 40 minutes or until the ribs are tender.

Pot Roast with Wine

Serves 8

1 onion, chopped
2 garlic cloves, chopped
1 (4-pound) rump roast
1/2 teaspoon rosemary

1/2 teaspoon thyme
2 teaspoons salt
1/4 teaspoon pepper
1 cup red wine

Sprinkle the onion and garlic in a slow cooker and place the roast in the cooker. Sprinkle the roast with the rosemary, thyme, salt and pepper. Pour the wine around the roast.

Cook on High for 5 hours or until the roast is very tender. Remove to a serving platter and pour the cooking liquid into a gravy boat to serve with the roast.

Hint: You can add chopped small red potatoes, carrots and/or celery about 1 hour before the end of the cooking time if desired.

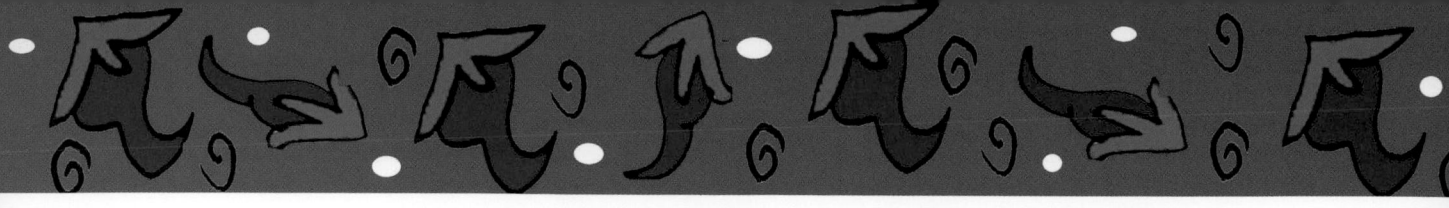

South African Meat Loaf

Serves 6 to 8

2 onions, coarsely chopped
1 garlic clove, crushed
3 tablespoons butter
2 pounds ground beef or
   ground lamb
1/2 cup chopped almonds
1/2 cup raisins
juice of 1/2 lemon
1 tablespoon vinegar

1 tablespoon sugar
2 tablespoons curry powder
1 tablespoon mixed herbs
1 teaspoon salt
pepper to taste
5 slices white bread
11/4 cups milk
2 eggs

Lots of lumber and thousands of volunteer hours have created a gathering place for the whole community. The Sunshine Playground, located on the grounds of the Long Center in the City of Clearwater, took sweat and heart for the members of the Junior League to provide a place for children to enjoy for years to come.

Sauté the onions and garlic in the butter in a skillet until golden brown. Spoon into a large mixing bowl. Add the ground beef, almonds, raisins, lemon juice, vinegar, sugar, curry powder, mixed herbs, salt and pepper and mix well.

Soak the bread in the milk in a bowl; press to remove the moisture, reserving about 3/4 cup milk. Add the bread and 1 egg to the meat mixture and mix well. Pack into a buttered shallow baking dish.

Beat the reserved milk with the remaining egg in a bowl. Pour over the meat loaf. Bake at 350 degrees for 1 hour or until the mixture is set and the top of the meat loaf is light brown.

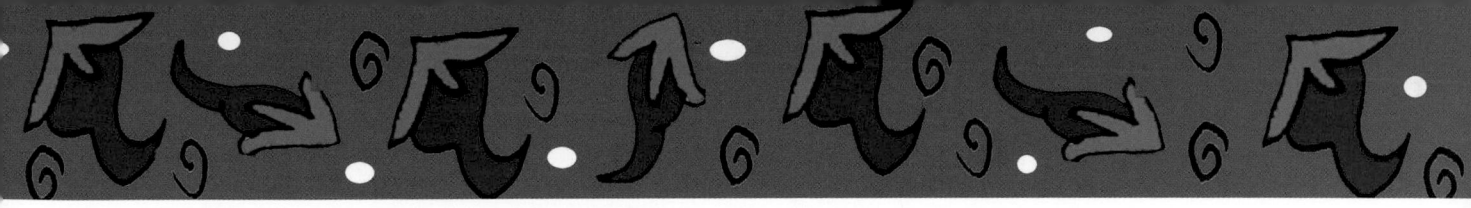

Lamb Paillarde Burger

Serves 4

Chef John Lewis at La Maison Gourmet generously donated his paillarde recipe.

4 (¼-inch) large red onion slices
olive oil
salt and pepper to taste
1 pound boneless leg of lamb

4 thin slices Gruyère cheese
4 Kaiser rolls
4 slices large ripe tomato
¼ cup balsamic vinegar

Preheat a grill or grill pan. Brush the onion slices with olive oil and sprinkle with salt and pepper. Grill for 2 minutes on each side.

Cut the lamb into 4 pieces and place between 2 sheets of plastic wrap. Pound ¼ inch thick with the flat side of a meat mallet. Brush with olive oil and sprinkle with salt and pepper. Grill for 2 minutes. Turn and top with the cheese and grill for 2 minutes longer.

Slice the rolls into halves horizontally. Brush the cut sides with olive oil. Place cut side down on the grill and grill until toasted. Layer the lamb, grilled onion slices and tomato slices on the bottom halves of the rolls. Drizzle with the balsamic vinegar and replace the roll tops. Serve warm.

Hint: Paillarde is a French term for a thin slice of meat pounded even thinner and then grilled.

Osso Buco

Serves 8

garlic-flavor olive oil, or a mixture
  of olive oil and 2 chopped
  garlic cloves
2 carrots, coarsely chopped
2 ribs celery, chopped
1 onion, chopped
8 (2-inch-thick) meaty veal shanks
flour
seasoned salt and freshly cracked
  pepper to taste

1 (28-ounce) can Italian tomatoes,
  coarsely chopped
1 (8-ounce) can tomato sauce
2 bay leaves
2 pinches of curry powder
2 1/2 cups (or more) water, chicken
  stock or red wine

Add enough olive oil to a heavy ovenproof 6-quart saucepan to cover the bottom. Heat over medium heat and add the carrots, celery and onion. Sauté for 5 minutes or until the onion is translucent. Remove to a bowl with a slotted spoon.

Coat the veal shanks with a mixture of flour, seasoned salt and pepper. Add 2 or 3 at a time to the saucepan, adding additional olive oil if needed. Cook until brown on all sides and remove to a bowl as they brown.

Arrange the veal shanks in a single layer in the saucepan. Add the sautéed vegetables, undrained tomatoes, tomato sauce, bay leaves and curry powder; adjust the pepper. Add enough of the water to cover the veal completely. Bring to a simmer and cover tightly.

Place in a 250-degree oven. Roast for 3 to 5 hours or until tender enough to fall from the bone, adding additional liquid as needed to cover. Discard the bay leaves and adjust the seasoning.

Serve over risotto, angel hair pasta or mashed potatoes. Add a green salad with a light vinaigrette and Italian bread to complete the meal.

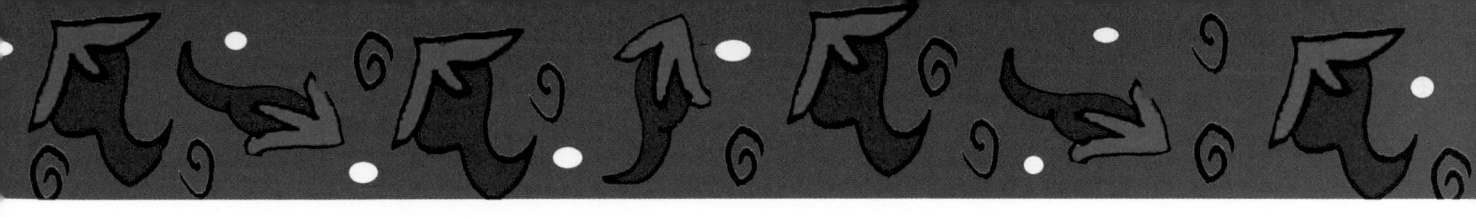

Apricot-Glazed Pork

Serves 6

½ cup apricot preserves
1 tablespoon Dijon mustard
1 tablespoon dried rosemary

½ teaspoon dried thyme
1 (2- to 2½-pound) rolled boneless
  pork loin

Combine the apricot preserves, mustard, rosemary and thyme in a small saucepan and mix well. Brush 1 tablespoon of the mixture over the pork loin. Place on a rack in a roasting pan sprayed with cooking spray. Insert a meat thermometer into the thickest portion.

Roast at 350 degrees for 1¾ hours or to 160 degrees on the meat thermometer, basting once with the apricot mixture. Let stand for 15 minutes before carving.

Bring the remaining apricot mixture to a boil in the saucepan. Reduce the heat and simmer for 2 minutes. Serve with the pork.

Sugared Cranberries

Makes 2 cups

2 cups water
1½ cups sugar

2 cups fresh cranberries
1 cup superfine sugar

Bring the water to a boil in a saucepan. Stir in 1½ cups sugar and reduce the heat, stirring to dissolve the sugar completely. Remove from the heat and stir in the cranberries. Let stand for 10 to 15 minutes. Spoon into a bowl and chill for 8 hours or longer. Drain, reserving the syrup for cocktails. Roll the cranberries in 1 cup superfine sugar in a shallow dish. Place in a single layer on a baking sheet and let stand until dry. Store in an airtight container. Serve with Apricot-Glazed Pork or fancy nuts and cocktails.

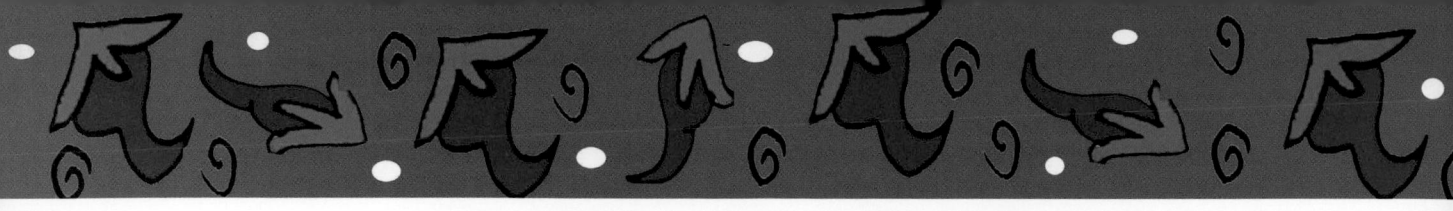

Florida Orange-Glazed Pork Chops

Serves 4

Pork Chops
4 (1-inch) pork chops
paprika, salt and pepper
　　to taste
1 tablespoon olive oil
1/2 cup water

Orange Glaze
2 tablespoons sugar
1 1/2 teaspoons cornstarch
1/4 teaspoon cinnamon
10 whole cloves
2 teaspoons grated
　　orange zest
1/2 cup freshly squeezed
　　orange juice

The Florida Botanical Gardens, in Largo, offers 182 acres that feature Florida plants in both natural and garden settings, including wildlife nesting habitats, restored wetlands, and natural bridges.

For the pork, sprinkle the chops with paprika, salt and pepper. Brown on both sides in the olive oil in a skillet. Reduce the heat and add the water. Simmer until cooked through, turning once and adding additional water if needed.

For the glaze, blend the sugar, cornstarch and cinnamon in a saucepan. Stir in the cloves, orange zest and orange juice. Cook until thickened and clear, stirring constantly. Remove the cloves and brush the glaze over the pork chops to serve. Garnish with orange slices and fresh parsley.

Hint: You can also brown the chops in an ovenproof skillet and bake at 350 degrees for 1 hour if preferred.

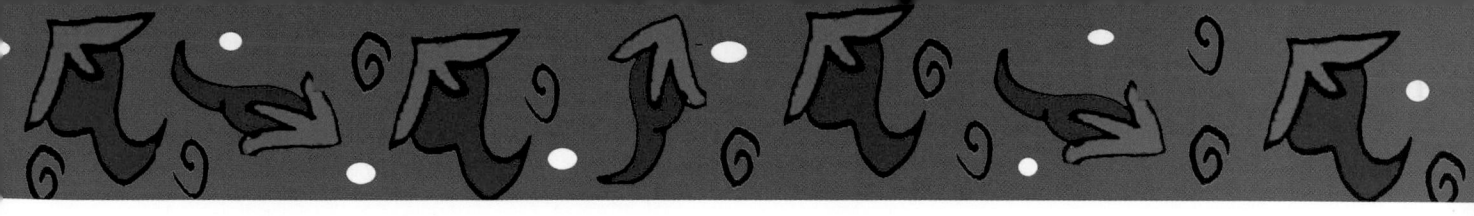

Grilled Pineapple Chicken

Serves 4

4 boneless skinless chicken breasts
1 cup canned crushed pineapple
1/4 cup soy sauce

1/4 cup dry sherry
1 tablespoon grated gingerroot
4 pineapple slices

Place the chicken between 2 sheets of waxed paper and pound 1/2 inch thick with a meat mallet. Combine the crushed pineapple, soy sauce, sherry and gingerroot in a bowl and mix well. Add the chicken and turn to coat well. Marinate in the refrigerator up to 12 hours.

Drain the chicken, reserving the marinade. Place the chicken and pineapple slices on the grill. Grill for 8 to 12 minutes or until the chicken is cooked through, turning once and basting with the reserved marinade. Serve on buns and garnish with chopped fresh cilantro.

Lemon and Rosemary Chicken

Serves 6

1 1/2 tablespoons chopped
   fresh rosemary
1/2 teaspoon garlic powder
3 tablespoons kosher salt

1/2 teaspoon pepper
1 (5- to 8-pound) chicken
3 lemons, cut into halves

Mix the rosemary, garlic powder, kosher salt and pepper in a small bowl, pressing the rosemary against the side of the bowl with the back of a spoon to release the flavor. Loosen the skin gently from the breast and thighs of the chicken and press the seasoning mixture carefully under the skin. Squeeze the lemon juice over the chicken and place the squeezed lemons in the cavity of the chicken.

Place in a roasting pan and cover with foil. Roast at 350 degrees for 20 to 23 minutes per pound or until the juices run clear, removing the foil during the last 30 minutes of roasting time. Let stand for 15 minutes before carving.

Gasparilla Drunken Chicken with Sweet Potato Mash

Serves 4

Local folklore contributed to the creation of this Belly Timbers Grill chicken recipe.

Gaspar the Pirate

Remnants of Florida's violent pirate past are seen coast to coast—but Tampa's Annual Gasparilla Pirate Festival celebrates that in a light-hearted way better than anywhere else. Legend says that José Gaspar navigated through Tampa Bay to take the key to the city and settle in Tampa, an event that has developed into a tradition that kicks off the festival's parade and activities each year.

4 (8-ounce) chicken breasts
Drunken Marinade (page 95)
flour for coating the chicken
salt and pepper to taste
1/4 cup (1/2 stick) butter
1 tablespoon flour
1 cup sweet white wine
1 cup chicken stock
Sweet Potato Mash (page 95)

Add chicken to the marinade and press the air out of the bag. Seal the bag and place in a bowl. Marinate in the refrigerator for 24 hours, turning occasionally.

Drain the chicken and pat dry with paper towels. Coat with flour seasoned with salt and pepper. Brown on all sides in the butter in an ovenproof sauté pan.

Bake, covered, at 350 degrees for 20 to 30 minutes or until tender when pierced with a fork. Remove to a platter and keep warm.

Drain most of the pan drippings from the sauté pan. Stir in 1 tablespoon flour and cook for 1 minute, stirring constantly. Stir in the wine. Simmer for 1 to 2 minutes, stirring constantly. Add the chicken stock and simmer until the sauce is thickened and reduced by 1/2, stirring constantly. Strain the sauce into a saucepan; reheat and adjust the seasonings. Serve the chicken with the sauce, seasonal vegetables and Sweet Potato Mash.

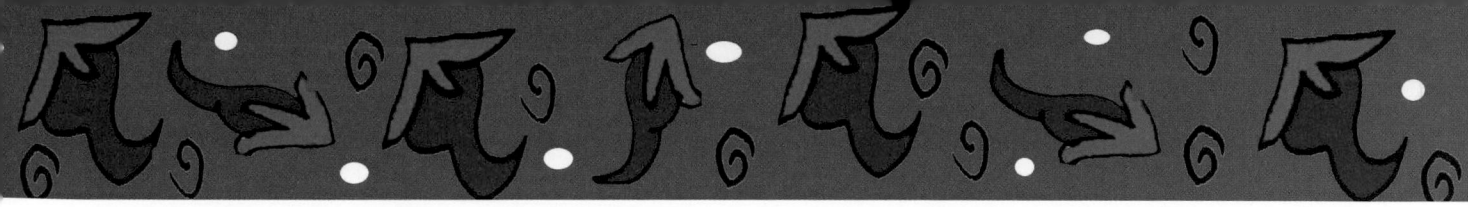

Drunken Marinade

Serves 4

½ cup rum
¼ cup bourbon
¼ cup brandy
1 cup teriyaki sauce
⅓ cup thawed frozen orange juice
    concentrate

1 carrot, grated
1 onion, grated
2 to 3 sprigs thyme
2 to 3 sprigs parsley

Combine the rum, bourbon, brandy, teriyaki sauce, orange juice concentrate, carrot, onion, thyme and parsley in a sealable plastic bag.

Sweet Potato Mash

Serves 8

8 large sweet potatoes
¼ cup packed brown sugar
3 tablespoons honey

1 teaspoon cinnamon
½ teaspoon nutmeg

Place the sweet potatoes in a baking pan. Bake at 350 degrees for 1 hour or until tender; cool and peel. Combine with the brown sugar, honey, cinnamon and nutmeg in a bowl and mash just until well mixed; the mixture may not be completely smooth.

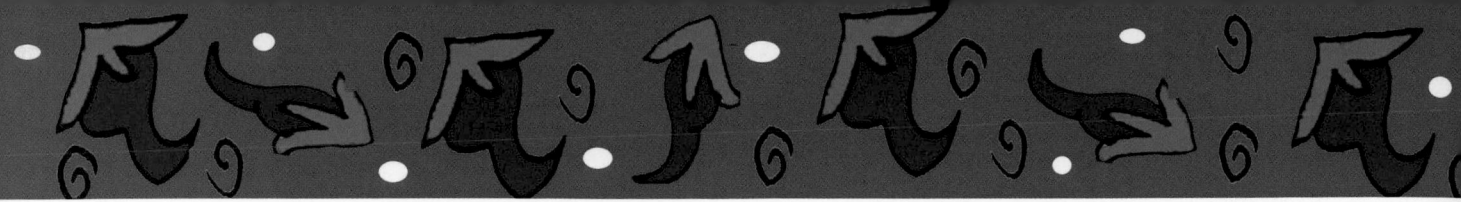

Chicken Scaloppine with Mango-Balsamic Sauce

Serves 4

This recipe came from "Spice of Life," a cooking demonstration at The Boca Raton Resort and Club. Andrew Roenbeck, the instructor, is the Executive Sous Chef there.

1/2 cup frozen mango purée, thawed
1/2 cup balsamic vinegar
2 tablespoons sugar
salt and black pepper to taste

4 boneless skinless chicken breasts
flour
1/4 cup olive oil

Combine the mango purée, balsamic vinegar, sugar, salt and pepper in a bowl and mix well. Pour half the mango mixture over the chicken into a shallow dish and turn the chicken to coat well. Reserve the remaining marinade mixture. Marinate the chicken in the refrigerator for 8 to 24 hours.

Remove the chicken from the marinade and discard the marinade. Coat the chicken with flour. Heat the olive oil in a large skillet. Add the chicken and cook until golden brown and cooked through, turning occasionally. Remove the chicken to a platter and keep warm. Add the reserved mango mixture to the pan and cook until the mixture is of a syrupy consistency, stirring frequently. Layer the chicken with Oven-Roasted Tomatoes (page 142) and drizzle with the mango syrup.

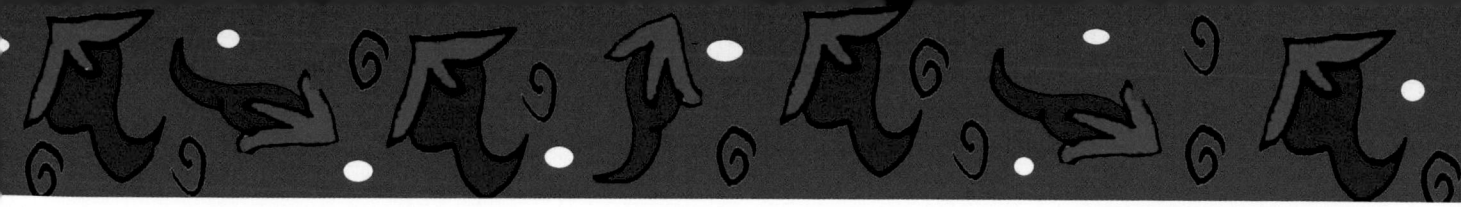

Elegant Penne

Serves 4

1¹/₂ tablespoons olive oil
4 to 6 vine-ripened tomatoes, chopped,
   or 1 (14-ounce) can chopped tomatoes
1 tablespoon minced garlic
¹/₄ teaspoon salt
¹/₄ teaspoon pepper
¹/₄ cup chopped fresh basil
8 ounces uncooked penne
³/₄ cup (3 ounces) crumbled feta cheese

Combine the olive oil, tomatoes, garlic, salt and pepper in a saucepan and cook until heated through. Add the basil. Cook over low heat for 5 minutes. Remove from the heat.

Cook the pasta in water in a 2-quart saucepan for 7 to 9 minutes or until tender; drain. Add to the tomato mixture. Add the cheese and mix gently.

Hint: The keys to the taste of this dish are to serve it warm or cold rather than hot to prevent the feta cheese from melting and to use only fresh basil.

A member of the National Register of Historic Places, Weedon Island Preserve, a rich mosaic of mangrove forest, open salt flats, pine flatwoods, and oak hammock, is 3,164 natural acres situated on Old Tampa Bay. The Cultural and National Historic Center features a creative blend of the Weedon Native American Indian culture and the natural environment.

Roasted Red Pepper Lasagna

Serves 8

Red Pepper Sauce
4 medium red bell peppers
 (about 1 1/2 pounds)
1 tablespoon olive oil
1 (28-ounce) can crushed tomatoes
1/2 cup chopped parsley
4 garlic cloves, crushed or minced
3/4 teaspoon pepper

Béchamel Sauce
1/3 cup butter or margarine
1/3 cup flour
1/2 teaspoon nutmeg
1/2 teaspoon salt
3 cups milk

Lasagna
12 no-boil lasagna noodles
1 1/4 cups (5 ounces) finely shredded
 Parmesan cheese

For the red pepper sauce, cut the bell peppers into halves, discarding the stems, seeds and membranes. Place cut side down on a foil-lined baking sheet. Roast at 425 degrees for 20 to 25 minutes or until the skins are bubbly and brown. Wrap the peppers in the foil and let stand for 20 to 30 minutes or until cool enough to handle. Peel off the skins and cut the peppers into strips.

Cook the peppers in the heated olive oil in a large saucepan over medium heat for 1 minute. Stir in the undrained tomatoes, parsley, garlic and pepper. Bring to a boil and reduce the heat. Simmer for 20 minutes, stirring frequently.

For the béchamel sauce, melt the butter in a medium saucepan. Stir in the flour, nutmeg and salt until smooth. Add the milk and cook over medium heat until thickened and bubbly, stirring constantly. Cook for 1 minute longer.

For the lasagna, arrange 3 noodles in a greased rectangular 3-quart baking dish, trimming as necessary to fit. Reserve 1/3 of the Parmesan cheese. Layer the red pepper sauce, béchamel sauce, remaining Parmesan cheese and noodles 1/2 at a time in the prepared baking dish. Top with the reserved Parmesan cheese.

Bake at 350 degrees for 30 to 35 minutes or until bubbly and light brown. Let stand for 10 minutes before serving.

Hint: You can assemble the dish in advance, cover with plastic wrap and refrigerate for up to 24 hours. To bake, replace the plastic wrap with foil and bake at 350 degrees for 30 minutes. Remove the foil and bake for 15 to 25 minutes longer or until bubbly.

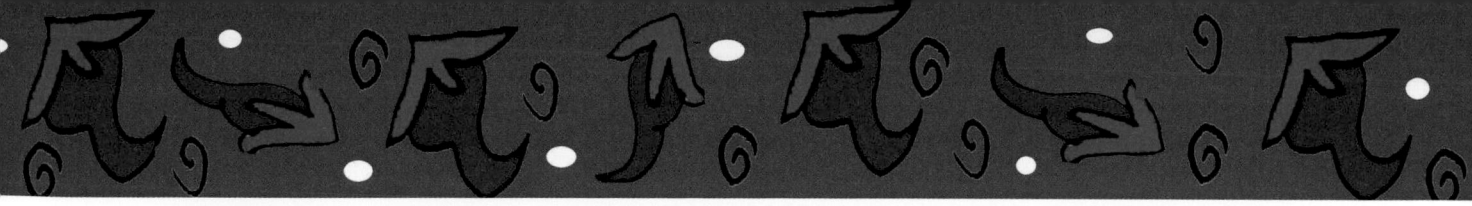

Polenta and Spinach Lasagna

Serves 4 to 6

Tomato Sauce
2 garlic cloves, finely chopped
2 tablespoons olive oil
8 ounces mushrooms,
    sliced 1/8 inch thick
2 tablespoons olive oil
2 garlic cloves, finely chopped
1/2 teaspoon chile flakes
1 (28-ounce) can whole tomatoes,
    chopped
3/4 teaspoon salt

Spinach
2 tablespoons olive oil
1 or 2 shallots, finely slivered
12 ounces fresh spinach
1/4 teaspoon salt

Lasagna
81/2 cups water
2 teaspoons salt
2 cups coarse-grain yellow cornmeal
1 cup (4 ounces) coarsely grated
    Parmigiano-Reggiano cheese
1/2 cup (2 ounces) chopped Fontina
    cheese
1 to 2 tablespoons unsalted butter

For the tomato sauce, sauté 2 garlic cloves in 2 tablespoons olive oil in a sauté pan over medium-high heat until golden brown. Add the mushrooms and sauté for 1 to 2 minutes. Remove to a bowl. Wipe out the sauté pan and add 2 tablespoons olive oil. Add 2 garlic cloves and the chile flakes. Sauté until the garlic is golden brown. Add the tomatoes and salt. Simmer for 20 to 30 minutes or until the desired consistency, stirring frequently. Add the mushrooms. Simmer for 3 minutes.

For the spinach, heat the olive oil in a large saucepan over high heat. Add the shallots and sauté for 1 to 2 minutes or until light brown. Add the spinach and sauté for 5 minutes, stirring constantly. Stir in the salt. Cool and chop the spinach.

For the lasagna, bring the water to a boil in a saucepan. Reduce the heat and stir in the salt. Add the cornmeal gradually and cook for 40 to 45 minutes or until the cornmeal polenta is thick and smooth, stirring constantly.

Spoon 1/3 of the cornmeal polenta into an 8×8-inch baking dish, spreading evenly with a wet spatula. Sprinkle with the Parmigiano-Reggiano cheese, spread with the spinach and sprinkle with the Fontina cheese. Spread half the remaining polenta in the dish and top with 3/4 of the tomato sauce. Add the remaining polenta and dot with the butter. Bake at 425 degrees for 45 minutes. Serve immediately with the remaining tomato sauce.

Grouper Florentine with
Blue Crab 102

Molasses Grouper 103

Pan-Seared Grouper in
Lemon Butter Sauce 103

Grilled Parmesan Grouper 104

Grouper Piccata 105

Grouper Romano 105

Grouper with Lime and
Tomato Garlic Sauce 106

Grilled Stuffed Whole Grouper 107

Grouper Stuffed with Shrimp and
Crab Meat au Gratin 108

Grouper Tempura 109

Beer-Battered Fish 109

Spicy Gingered Grouper Sauce 109

Bold and Spicy Tartar Sauce 110

Southern Catfish 110

Grilled Halibut Hoisin with
Peaches 111

Mango Salsa 111

Mahi Mahi with Spinach and
Feta Cheese 112

Mustard-Maple Salmon 112

Pistachio Cream Cheese
Crusted Salmon 113

Salmon en Croûte with
Spinach and Mushrooms 114, 115

Vodka Sauce 115

Roasted Red Snapper with
Lively Red Salsa 116

Pescado à la Veracruzana 117

Brie Crab Cakes with
Dill-Lime Mustard Sauce 118

Soft-Shell Blue Crabs with
Mustard Sauce 119

Lobster Cakes with
Tomato Ginger Jam 120

Seared Scallops Over
Baby Spinach 121

Sea Scallops in Vermouth 122

Shrimp and Artichokes 123

Barbecued Shrimp 124

Oven-Barbecued Shrimp 125

Firecracker Shrimp 125

Clearwater Boil 126

Creole Jambalaya 127

from the
Sea

Grouper Florentine with Blue Crab

Serves 6

The Salt Rock Grill's Chef Barry Spaulding has created a new experience for beach diners. It's not all flip-flops and swim suits on the Gulf beaches anymore.

Florentine Sauce

3 tablespoons chopped garlic
3 tablespoons chopped shallots
clarified butter
1/4 cup sherry
10 ounces fresh spinach, lightly
    steamed and chopped
2 cups heavy cream
1/2 teaspoon Tabasco sauce
1 teaspoon salt
1/2 teaspoon pepper
1/3 cup cornstarch
1/2 cup water
8 ounces blue crab claw meat,
    cooked

Grouper

6 (8- to 9-ounce) grouper fillets
salt and pepper to taste
flour
clarified butter
1/4 cup Chablis
1 tablespoon chopped parsley
1/4 cup Parmesan cheese

For the sauce, sauté the garlic and shallots in a small amount of clarified butter in a sauté pan until wilted. Add the sherry, stirring to deglaze the pan. Stir in the spinach, cream, Tabasco sauce, salt and pepper. Simmer for 8 minutes.

Dissolve the cornstarch in the water in a bowl. Bring the sauce to a low boil and stir in the cornstarch mixture. Cook for 1 minute or until thickened, stirring constantly. Stir in the crab meat. Keep warm.

For the grouper, sprinkle the fillets with salt and pepper and coat lightly with flour. Sauté in clarified butter in a sauté pan until golden brown. Add the wine and parsley. Cover and steam for 2 to 3 minutes or until the fish flakes easily. Ladle the sauce over the top to serve. Sprinkle with Parmesan cheese.

Chef's Tip: Overcooking seafood is a common problem. In order to determine when fin fish are done, insert the tip of a fork into the thickest part of the fish, count to ten and remove the fork. If the tines are very warm, the fish is done.

Molasses Grouper

Serves 8 to 12

1/4 cup molasses
1/2 cup Merlot wine
juice of 1 lemon
1/4 cup Old Bay seasoning

1 tablespoon finely chopped cilantro
1 tablespoon white pepper
8 to 12 grouper fillets
sesame oil or olive oil

Combine the molasses, wine, lemon juice, Old Bay seasoning, white pepper and cilantro in a bowl and mix well. Add the grouper fillets and turn the fish to coat well. Marinate in the refrigerator for 40 minutes, turning once. Drain the fillets and brush both sides with sesame oil. Grill over medium-high heat for 3 to 4 minutes on each side or just until the fish flakes easily; do not overcook.

Pan-Seared Grouper in Lemon Butter Sauce

Serves 4

Compliments of the Westin Innisbrook Resort

Grouper
4 (6-ounce) grouper fillets
salt and pepper to taste
1 cup flour
1/4 cup olive oil
1/4 cup (1/2 stick) butter

Lemon Butter Sauce
1 cup sliced onion
1 cup sliced button mushrooms
1/4 cup olive oil
1 garlic clove, chopped
juice of 1 lemon
1 cup white wine
1/4 cup (1/2 stick) butter
salt and pepper to taste

For the grouper, season the fillets with salt and pepper and coat with the flour. Heat the olive oil and butter in a sauté pan and add the grouper fillets. Sear on both sides until light brown. Remove to a baking sheet. Bake at 325 degrees for 15 minutes or until cooked through.

For the sauce, sauté the onion and mushrooms in the olive oil in a sauté pan for 5 minutes. Add the garlic and sauté for 1 minute. Stir in the lemon juice and wine. Cook until reduced by half. Remove from the heat. Whisk in the butter and season with salt and pepper. Serve with the fish. Garnish with basil.

Grilled Parmesan Grouper

Serves 4

1 1/2 tablespoons grated Parmesan cheese
1/2 cup olive oil
1 tablespoon minced onion
3/4 teaspoon sugar
3/4 teaspoon dried basil leaves
3/4 teaspoon dried oregano leaves

3/4 teaspoon dry mustard
2 teaspoons salt
3/4 teaspoon pepper
1/4 cup red wine vinegar
1 tablespoon lemon juice
1 (2-pound) grouper fillet, 1 1/2 to 2 inches thick

Combine the Parmesan cheese, olive oil, onion, sugar, basil, oregano, dry mustard, salt and pepper in a blender and process for 30 seconds. Add the vinegar and lemon juice and process for 30 seconds longer.

Place the grouper in a fish grilling basket. Grill for 10 minutes on each side or until the fish flakes easily, basting frequently with the sauce.

 **Chef's Tip:** To avoid seafood sticking to the grill, soak a paper towel in vegetable oil for a few seconds, then brush it across the top of the grill using tongs.

Grouper Piccata

Serves 2

*The Pappas name is synonymous with fine dining in Pinellas County, and Nick Pappas'
Grillmarks lives up to the reputation.*

2 (8-ounce) grouper fillets
flour
4 tablespoons olive oil
1/2 cup white wine
juice of 1 lemon

1/2 cup (1 stick) butter, sliced
2 tablespoons capers
2 teaspoons minced garlic
2 teaspoons minced shallot
salt and pepper to taste

Coat the grouper lightly with flour. Heat the olive oil in a sauté pan and add the
fish. Sauté for 3 to 5 minutes on each side or until cooked through. Remove
to a platter.

Add the wine to the sauté pan, stirring to deglaze. Cook until reduced by
1/2. Stir in the lemon juice and cook until reduced by 1/4. Add the butter, capers,
garlic and shallot and mix well. Simmer for 2 minutes. Season with salt and
pepper. Serve with the fish.

Grouper Romano

Serves 4

Compliments of the Westin Innisbrook Resort

4 (6-ounce) grouper fillets
salt and pepper to taste
2 tomatoes, chopped
2 tablespoons chopped fresh basil

1/2 cup (2 ounces) grated Romano
    cheese
1/2 cup (1 stick) butter, melted
lemon wedges

Season the grouper with salt and pepper and place on a baking sheet. Top with
the tomatoes, basil and cheese; drizzle with the butter.

Bake at 350 degrees for 15 to 20 minutes or until the fish flakes easily. Serve
with fresh lemon wedges.

Grouper with Lime and Tomato Garlic Sauce

Serves 4

Bonefish Grill has become famous nationally for its generous helpings of savory seafood.

Lime and Tomato Garlic Sauce

1/2 cup coarsely chopped sun-dried tomatoes
1/2 cup coarsely chopped fresh tomatoes
1/4 cup chopped garlic
1/2 cup white wine
1/4 cup lemon juice
1/4 cup lime juice
2 tablespoons sugar
1 cup heavy cream
2 tablespoons butter, chopped
2 teaspoons salt
1 teaspoon white pepper

Grouper

1 (2-pound) grouper fillet
seafood seasoning to taste
melted butter
1 cup sautéed spinach
4 ounces lump crab meat

More than 300 varieties of fish swim in the Gulf of Mexico and Tampa Bay, including grouper, snapper, trout, snook, tarpon, red fish, kingfish, shark, sailfish, and mackerel. Mangroves, sea grasses, reefs, and even piers are habitats for these fish.

For the sauce, combine the sun-dried tomatoes, fresh tomatoes, garlic, wine, lemon juice, lime juice and sugar in a saucepan. Cook until reduced by 1/2. Add the cream and cook until thickened; do not boil.

Reduce the heat to medium to low and add the butter gradually, stirring to incorporate well. Remove from the heat and season with salt and white pepper. Keep warm.

For the grouper, season the fillet with seafood seasoning and drizzle with butter. Place on an oiled grill and grill until the fish flakes easily.

Place the fish on serving plates and top with the spinach and crab meat. Spoon the sauce over the top.

Grilled Stuffed Whole Grouper

Serves 8

1 (10- to 12-pound) black grouper or red grouper
1 large onion, chopped
10 to 12 garlic cloves, chopped
2 each yellow squash and zucchini, cut into halves and sliced
12 cherry tomatoes, cut into halves
1 pound asparagus, chopped
1/4 cup virgin olive oil
2 tablespoons mayonnaise
1/3 cup rum
3 tablespoons Old Bay seasoning
1 teaspoon thyme
1 tablespoon crushed bay leaves
1 tablespoon salt
1 1/2 tablespoons black pepper
1 teaspoon cayenne pepper
1 1/2 pounds blue crab or back fin lump crab meat
olive oil
kosher salt
sliced aged Swiss cheese, or other strong-flavored cheese

Place a sharp knife on the back of the fish behind the gill plate and cut down the back along 1 side of the backbone, cutting to but not through the skin of the belly. Repeat the process on the other side of the backbone. Remove and discard the backbone, ribs and entrails, reaching into the throat to remove the liver and heart if possible; leave the head and tail intact. Rinse well.

Combine the onion, garlic, yellow squash, zucchini, cherry tomatoes and asparagus in a large bowl. Add 1/4 cup olive oil, the mayonnaise, rum, Old Bay seasoning, thyme, bay leaves, salt, black pepper and cayenne pepper and mix well.

Spoon the vegetable mixture and crab meat into the cavity of the fish, beginning at the head and pouring any remaining liquid over the stuffing. Sew the cavity closed with baker's twine. Rub the fish with additional olive oil and sprinkle with kosher salt.

Wrap the fish with foil and grill for 1 1/2 to 2 hours or to 160 to 165 degrees internally. Place on a serving platter and remove the twine. Open the fish and layer the Swiss cheese over the stuffing. Garnish with Parmesan cheese and chopped parsley.

Pinellas County averages 361 days of sunshine per year, with an average temperature in the mid-seventies, making outdoor dining a year-round tradition. Beach picnics, sunset boat cruises, kayaking to an unspoiled island, and neighborhood barbecues all make entertaining unique in the Clearwater-Dunedin community.

Grouper Stuffed with Shrimp and Crab Meat au Gratin

Serves 4 to 6

Kally K's in Dunedin offers family-style dining in a comfortable atmosphere, all while serving gourmet meals!

¹/4 cup (¹/2 stick) butter
¹/2 cup flour
2 cups milk
1 teaspoon chicken base
¹/2 teaspoon garlic powder
1 cup (4 ounces) grated Parmesan
  cheese

1 cup shredded crab meat
¹/2 cup cooked baby shrimp
2 (9- to 10-ounce) grouper fillets
salt and pepper to taste
vegetable oil
paprika to taste
¹/2 cup water

Bring the butter to a simmer in a saucepan. Remove from the heat and add the flour, whisking until thickened. Add the milk, chicken base and garlic powder and cook over medium heat. Add all but 1 tablespoon of the Parmesan cheese and cook until thickened, stirring constantly. Remove from the heat and stir in the crab meat and shrimp. Chill for 1 hour.

Cut the grouper fillets into halves and season with salt and pepper. Spoon the crab meat mixture onto half the grouper pieces and top with the remaining grouper pieces, pressing lightly. Arrange in a baking dish.

Drizzle the grouper with oil; sprinkle with paprika, salt, pepper and the reserved Parmesan cheese. Add the water to the baking dish. Bake at 400 degrees for 20 to 25 minutes or until golden brown.

Grouper Tempura

Serves 6

1/2 cup flour
1/2 cup cornstarch
1 teaspoon baking powder
1/2 teaspoon baking soda
1/4 teaspoon salt
1 egg

2/3 cup ice water
6 grouper fillets
vegetable oil for deep-frying
Spicy Gingered Grouper
 Sauce (sidebar)

Mix the flour, cornstarch, baking powder, baking soda and salt in a bowl. Whisk the egg and ice water in a bowl until blended and stir into the flour mixture.

Coat the fillets with the batter and deep-fry in hot oil in a skillet just until golden brown; drain. Serve with Spicy Gingered Grouper Sauce.

Beer-Battered Fish

Serves 10

3 pounds grouper or other
 firm white fish, cut into
 strips
1 (16-ounce) bottle of French
 salad dressing
1 1/2 cups flour

4 cups Bisquick
2 teaspoons baking powder
4 eggs, beaten
2 cups beer
vegetable oil for deep-frying

Combine the fish and the salad dressing in a shallow dish, turning to coat well. Marinate, covered, in the refrigerator for 6 hours; drain. Coat with the flour.

Combine the Bisquick, baking powder, eggs and beer in a mixing bowl and mix well. Heat oil to 375 degrees in a deep fryer. Dip the fish into the beer mixture and deep-fry in the oil for 4 minutes or until golden brown on all sides. Drain on paper towels and serve with lemon wedges and malt vinegar or Bold and Spicy Tartar Sauce (page 110).

Spicy Gingered Grouper Sauce

Combine 1/3 cup minced scallions, 1/3 cup minced fresh gingerroot, 1/4 cup minced mushrooms, 1 minced jalapeño chile, 1/2 cup water, 1/3 cup sugar, 3 tablespoons ketchup, 1/3 cup white vinegar, and 1 teaspoon sesame oil in a saucepan and mix well. Bring just to a boil and stir in a mixture of 1 teaspoon water and 1/2 teaspoon cornstarch. Cook until thickened, stirring frequently. Also serve with monkfish, mahi mahi, or orange roughy.

Southern Catfish

Bold and Spicy Tartar Sauce

Combine 2 cups mayonnaise with 1/2 cup chopped dill pickles and 1 tablespoon spicy brown mustard, the juice of half of a lemon and 1/4 to 1/2 teaspoon each cayenne pepper, black pepper, garlic powder and red pepper flakes in a bowl; mix well. Chill in the refrigerator for 8 hours or longer. Serve with fried fish. Makes 2 1/2 cups.

Anchovy Garlic Sauce

1 cup homemade chicken stock
2 tablespoons anchovy paste
3 tablespoons sliced garlic
salt to taste
1 jalapeño chile, seeded and sliced
2 tablespoons finely chopped parsley

Catfish

8 ounces catfish fillets
3 eggs, beaten
flour
canola oil
1 teaspoon butter
grated Parmesan cheese

For the sauce, combine the chicken stock and anchovy paste in a small saucepan and cook until reduced to the desired consistency. Add the garlic and cook for 4 minutes. Season with salt. Add the jalapeño chile and parsley and keep warm over very low heat.

For the catfish, dip the fillets into the eggs and coat lightly with flour. Sauté in a small amount of canola oil and 1 teaspoon butter in a nonstick skillet until light brown on both sides.

Remove to a serving plate and spoon the sauce over the top. Sprinkle with Parmesan cheese. You may try grouper or trout instead of the catfish if desired.

Grilled Halibut Hoisin with Peaches   Serves 6

¹/4 cup hoisin sauce
¹/4 cup orange juice
1 to 2 peaches, chopped
2 tablespoons chopped fresh
    cilantro
1 tablespoon shredded or
    minced fresh gingerroot

1 tablespoon Mirin
1 teaspoon olive oil
¹/4 teaspoon chili powder, or
    1 small jalapeño chile,
    minced
salt to taste
2 pounds halibut or
    mahi mahi steaks

Combine the hoisin sauce, orange juice, peaches, cilantro, gingerroot, Mirin, olive oil, chili powder and salt in a bowl and mix well. Spoon the hoisin sauce mixture over the halibut in a shallow dish, turning to coat. Marinate in the refrigerator for 30 minutes, turning occasionally.

Form 2 trays with sides using 2 layers of heavy-duty foil. Drain the halibut, reserving the marinade. Arrange the halibut on the foil trays. Grill over hot coals for 5 minutes and turn. Spoon the reserved marinade over the halibut and grill for 4 to 6 minutes longer or until the halibut flakes easily. Serve immediately with bok choy and mango couscous or your favorite Asian vegetables.

 **Chef's Tip:** Mirin is Japanese wine found in Asian food markets.

Mango Salsa

Chop 2 mangos and 1 avocado and combine in a bowl. Add ¹/4 cup finely chopped red onion, ¹/4 cup finely chopped red bell pepper, 3 tablespoons finely chopped cilantro, 1 seeded and chopped jalapeño chile, ¹/4 cup orange juice, 1 tablespoon olive oil and 1 tablespoon lime juice. Mix well; store in the refrigerator. Makes 3 cups.

Mahi Mahi with Spinach and Feta Cheese

Serves 4

24 ounces frozen spinach, thawed
3 tablespoons chopped garlic
salt and pepper to taste

1 (1½-pound) mahi mahi fillet
6 ounces feta cheese, crumbled

Sauté the spinach with the garlic in a nonstick skillet. Season with salt and pepper. Arrange the mahi mahi skin side down in a baking dish. Spread the spinach evenly over the top and sprinkle with the cheese. Bake at 375 degrees for 15 to 20 minutes or until the mahi mahi flakes easily.

Chef's Tip: Try this recipe using other types of mild white fish.

Mustard-Maple Salmon

Serves 4

3 tablespoons Dijon mustard
3 tablespoons maple syrup
1 tablespoon balsamic vinegar
¼ teaspoon sea salt

⅛ teaspoon freshly ground pepper
4 (6-ounce) salmon fillets,
  1 inch thick

Combine the mustard, syrup, balsamic vinegar, sea salt and pepper in a resealable plastic bag. Add the salmon and seal tightly. Turn to coat. Marinate in the refrigerator for 20 minutes, turning occasionally.

Drain the salmon, reserving the marinade. Arrange the salmon on a grill rack or broiler rack sprayed with nonstick cooking spray. Grill over hot coals or broil for 6 minutes per side or until the salmon flakes easily, basting with the reserved marinade occasionally. Serve immediately.

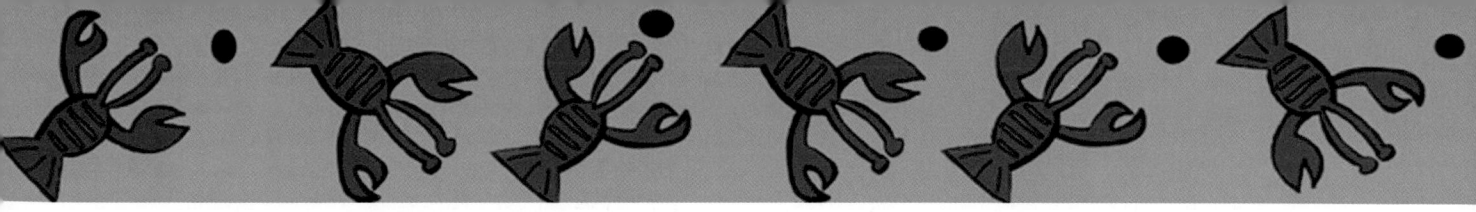

Pistachio Cream Cheese Crusted Salmon

Serves 4

²/3 cup finely chopped
  pistachios
¹/3 cup seasoned bread
  crumbs
8 ounces cream cheese,
  softened
¹/2 teaspoon finely chopped
  fresh rosemary, or
  ¹/4 teaspoon dried rosemary

¹/2 teaspoon finely chopped
  fresh thyme, or
  ¹/2 teaspoon dried thyme
5 tablespoons Dijon mustard
3 drops of Tabasco sauce
4 (5-ounce) salmon fillets,
  skin removed and
  patted dry

Mix the pistachios and bread crumbs in a bowl. Process the cream cheese, rosemary, thyme, mustard and Tabasco sauce in a food processor until combined.

Coat the fillets with the cream cheese mixture. If the fillets are thick, just coat the top and sides. Roll in the pistachio mixture and pat lightly. Arrange the fillets on a nonstick baking sheet and bake at 375 degrees on the center oven rack for 10 to 12 minutes or until the fillets flake easily.

The largest fishing fleet on the west coast of Florida makes its home at the Clearwater Marina. Berthed in the marina are boats that offer a myriad of activities: fishing, sightseeing, sailing, dining and dancing, parasailing, "hands-on" marine life adventures, and more.

Salmon en Croûte with Spinach and Mushrooms

Spinach and Mushroom Filling

1 (10-ounce) package frozen chopped
  spinach, thawed and drained
1 tablespoon olive oil
1 tablespoon butter
1/4 cup finely chopped onion
8 ounces button mushrooms,
  chopped
salt and pepper to taste

Salmon

4 (4-ounce) salmon fillets
2 teaspoons dried dill weed, or
  2 tablespoons chopped fresh
  dill weed
salt and pepper to taste
1 tablespoon fresh lemon juice
2 tablespoons olive oil
1 tablespoon butter
1 sheet frozen puff pastry, thawed
1 egg, beaten
1 tablespoon water
Vodka Sauce (page 115)

For the filling, press the excess moisture from the spinach. Heat the olive oil and butter in a skillet over medium-high heat. Sauté the onion in the oil mixture until almost tender. Stir in the spinach, mushrooms, salt and pepper. Cool slightly. You may substitute 16 ounces steamed squeezed dry fresh spinach for the frozen spinach.

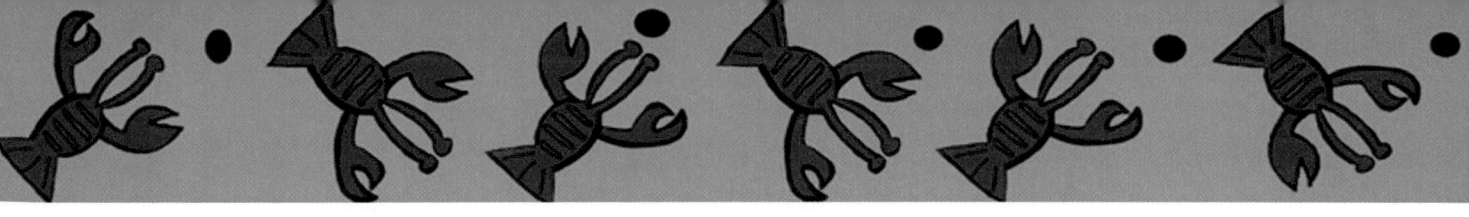

For the salmon, sprinkle both sides of the salmon with the dill weed, salt and pepper. Drizzle the lemon juice over the flesh side. Heat a skillet over medium-high heat and add the olive oil and butter. Heat until the oil mixture is hot and add the salmon skin side up. Cook for 3 minutes or until brown. Turn and sear the skin side for 2 minutes. Remove to a platter and chill, covered, in the refrigerator.

Thaw the pastry for 20 minutes. Roll the pastry into a 14×14-inch square on a lightly floured surface and cut into 4 equal squares. Top each fillet with 1/4 of the filling and arrange each fillet on 1 pastry square. Brush the edges of the pastry with a mixture of the egg and water. Bring the opposite corners over the top of the salmon to cover and pinch the edges to seal. Arrange seam side down on an ungreased baking sheet.

Brush the tops of the pastry with the remaining egg wash and bake at 400 degrees for 20 to 25 minutes or until golden brown. Serve with the Vodka Sauce (at right) or your favorite dill sauce. You may substitute 1 (1-pound) salmon fillet for 4 (4-ounce) fillets.

Hint: Spoon Vodka Sauce on individual plates or on a serving platter. Arrange the fillets or fillet over the sauce. Any remaining Spinach and Mushroom Filling may be served on the side. Garnish with sprigs of fresh dill weed.

Vodka Sauce

Sauté 1 tablespoon chopped onion in 1 tablespoon butter in a skillet until tender. Stir in 1/4 cup white wine. Cook until reduced, stirring frequently. Stir in 1 cup fish stock and 1/4 cup vodka. Bring to a boil and boil for 15 minutes, stirring occasionally. Stir in 1/2 cup cream. Add 1/16 teaspoon cornstarch and mix well. Cook until thickened and season with salt and pepper.

Roasted Red Snapper with Lively Red Salsa

Serves 4

Lively Red Salsa
2 large ripe tomatoes, chopped
2 tablespoons chopped scallions
2 tablespoons chopped fresh cilantro
1 tablespoon olive oil
2 teaspoons finely minced garlic
2 teaspoons fresh lime juice
salt and freshly ground pepper to taste

Red Snapper
2 tablespoons extra-virgin olive oil
1 tablespoon fresh lime juice
1 tablespoon chopped fresh cilantro
4 (8-ounce) red snapper fillets
salt and freshly ground pepper to taste

The Taste of Clearwater, held each September, is a wonderful way to sample cuisine from over 50 local restaurants. The Clearwater Regional Chamber of Commerce has been hosting this event for over 20 years.

For the salsa, combine the tomatoes, scallions, cilantro, olive oil, garlic and lime juice in a bowl and mix gently. Season with salt and pepper.

For the red snapper, whisk the olive oil, lime juice and cilantro in a small bowl. Arrange the fillets skin side down on a lightly oiled baking sheet. Brush with the cilantro mixture and sprinkle with salt and pepper. Let stand at room temperature for 15 minutes.

Bake at 400 degrees for 30 minutes or just until the fillets flake easily. Arrange the fillets on a serving platter and top each with some of the salsa. Serve immediately.

Pescado à la Veracruzana

Serves 10

Casa Tina brings flavorful, healthy Mexican food—and this delicious sauce—to the area in a quaint bistro atmosphere.

1 small onion, chopped
1 tablespoon olive oil
5 ripe tomatoes, chopped
2 pickled jalapeño chiles, chopped
1 bunch parsley, trimmed and finely chopped
½ cup capers
½ cup pimento-stuffed olives
salt to taste
10 grouper fillets

Sauté the onion in the olive oil in a skillet for 5 minutes. Add the tomatoes, jalapeño chiles, parsley, capers and olives in the order listed and mix well. Cook for a few minutes to allow the flavors to blend, stirring frequently. Season with salt.

Place the grouper on an oiled grill or in a grill basket and grill over hot coals until the fish flakes easily with a fork. Remove the grouper to dinner plates and top with the sauce.

Originally started as art classes given by League members, the Dunedin Fine Arts and Cultural Center offers fine art and classes to the community. It also serves as host for the annual Art Harvest, one of the largest fine art festivals in the Southeast, held each fall at Highlander Park.

Brie Crab Cakes with Dill-Lime Mustard Sauce

Makes 6 crab cakes

Dill-Lime Mustard Sauce

4 ounces Dijon mustard
8 ounces mayonnaise
juice of 3 limes
chopped fresh dill weed to taste
salt and pepper to taste

Crab Cakes and Assembly

1/2 red bell pepper, finely chopped
1/2 yellow bell pepper, finely chopped
2 tablespoons chopped shallots
2 garlic cloves, minced
1 tablespoon olive oil
16 ounces fresh lump or back fin
   crab meat, or a combination of
   both, drained and shells removed
1 cup bread crumbs
1 egg, beaten
chopped fresh herbs to taste, such as
   basil, parsley and chives
6 ounces Brie cheese, chilled,
   rind removed and chopped
salt and pepper to taste
flour
3 tablespoons olive oil
baby salad greens

For the sauce, combine the mustard, mayonnaise, lime juice, dill weed, salt and pepper in a bowl and mix well. Chill, covered, in the refrigerator until serving time.

For the crab cakes, sauté the bell peppers, shallots and garlic in 1 tablespoon olive oil in a saucepan until most of the oil is absorbed. Let stand until cool. Combine the sautéed bell pepper mixture, crab meat, bread crumbs, egg and herbs in a bowl and mix gently. Stir in the cheese and season with salt and pepper. Chill, covered, for 1 hour.

Shape the crab meat mixture into 6 large cakes and coat with flour. Sauté the cakes in 3 tablespoons olive oil in a skillet until golden brown on both sides; drain. Mound salad greens on each of 6 dinner plates and top each with 1 crab cake. Drizzle with the sauce.

118

Soft-Shell Blue Crabs with Mustard Sauce

Serves 4

Mustard Sauce
2 teaspoons butter or margarine
1/2 cup sour cream
1 1/2 tablespoons Creole mustard
1/2 teaspoon parsley flakes
1/8 teaspoon salt

Soft Shell Crabs
8 live soft shell crabs
1 cup flour
1 teaspoon salt
1/4 teaspoon pepper
1/8 teaspoon paprika (optional)
vegetable oil for frying
mixed salad greens
lemon wedges

For the sauce, heat the butter in a double boiler until melted. Stir in the sour cream, mustard, parsley flakes and salt. Simmer over low heat until heated through, stirring occasionally; do not boil. Vary the flavor of the sauce by incorporating different kinds of mustards.

For the crabs, clean the crabs by cutting off the eyes with kitchen shears across the face of the crab. Remove the mouth. Lift the points of the crab shell and remove the sandbags and gills. Turn the crab and remove the apron at the lower part of the shell. Rinse and pat dry.

Mix the flour, salt, pepper and paprika in a shallow dish. Coat the crabs with the flour mixture and tap to remove the excess. Fry the crabs in oil in a skillet for 3 to 5 minutes or until golden brown, turning once; drain. Serve the crabs over salad greens with the Mustard Sauce or Roasted Red Pepper Sauce (page 42) and lemon wedges.

Pinellas County's annual October Stone Crab Festival celebrates the locals' favorite treat. It is unlawful to harvest, possess, or sell any stone crab claw that has a forearm length of less than two and three-fourths inches. Stone crab claws are removed one at a time when harvested. The claws grow back in approximately eighteen months, allowing us to enjoy their delectable claws year after year. Stone crabs are available from October until May and are truly worth the wait.

Lobster Cakes with Tomato Ginger Jam

Serves 2 to 3

The Lobster Pot of Redington Shores stands prominently on Gulf Boulevard. Chef Steve Peek offers his favorite lobster dish.

Tomato Ginger Jam

2 shallots, minced
3 tablespoons minced fresh
  gingerroot
1 teaspoon minced garlic
3 tablespoons butter
5 tomatoes, seeded and chopped
3/4 cup sugar

Lobster Cakes

1 cup unseasoned bread crumbs
1 tablespoon Old Bay seasoning
1 teaspoon dry mustard
1 pound lobster meat, cooked and
  cut into 1/2-inch pieces
2 tablespoons chopped fresh parsley
1 cup mayonnaise
2 egg yolks, beaten
1 tablespoon Worcestershire sauce
vegetable oil or butter for frying

For the jam, sauté the shallots, gingerroot and garlic in the butter in a saucepan. Stir in the tomatoes and sugar. Cook until thickened, stirring frequently. Spoon into a bowl and chill, covered, in the refrigerator.

For the cakes, combine the bread crumbs, Old Bay seasoning and dry mustard in a bowl and mix well. Add the lobster meat and parsley to the bread crumb mixture and toss to combine. Mix the mayonnaise, egg yolks and Worcestershire sauce in a bowl and stir into the lobster mixture. Shape the lobster mixture into cakes and pan-fry in oil in a skillet until brown on both sides; drain. Top each cake with 1 teaspoon of the jam.

Seared Scallops Over Baby Spinach

1 to 1½ pounds sea scallops
Cajun seasoning to taste
olive oil
¼ cup minced garlic
20 ounces baby spinach
lemon wedges

Line a plate with 2 paper towels. Pat the scallops dry and arrange in a single layer on the prepared plate. Sprinkle 1 side lightly with Cajun seasoning.

Add enough olive oil to 2 separate skillets to cover the bottoms. Heat the oil in 1 of the skillets over medium-high heat and add the garlic. Sauté until the garlic just begins to brown. Add the spinach and sauté until wilted. Immediately begin to heat the remaining skillet over high heat until the oil is hot enough to sizzle a couple of drops of water. Add the scallops to the hot oil seasoned side down and sprinkle the remaining side lightly with Cajun seasoning. Sear on both sides. Serve seared scallops over sautéed baby spinach and garlic. Serve with lemon wedges.

Clearwater Beach has been consistently named one of the Top 10 Beaches in the United States by USATODAY.com. In 2001, this beach took the honor as the "Best City Beach on the Gulf of Mexico" according to Dr. Stephen Leatherman ("Dr. Beach") and Condé Nast Traveler.

Sea Scallops in Vermouth

Serves 2 to 4

Home chefs take advantage of the fresh fish available at Ward's Seafood Market & Galley. Ward's also provides a variety of recipes in case you're wondering how to prepare that beautiful piece of fish.

2 tablespoons extra-virgin olive oil
1 shallot, chopped
2 (14-ounce) cans water-pack
  artichoke quarters, drained
Salt and pepper to taste

1/4 cup fresh parsley leaves, chopped
2 tablespoons drained capers
16 sea scallops, drained and trimmed
1 tablespoon extra-virgin olive oil
1/2 cup dry vermouth

Heat a large nonstick skillet over medium heat. Add 2 tablespoons olive oil and the shallot to the hot skillet and cook for 1 minute, stirring frequently. Add the artichokes and toss to combine. Cook just until heated through, stirring constantly. Season with salt and pepper and stir in the parsley and capers. Spoon the artichoke mixture into a serving bowl.

Wipe the skillet with a paper towel and return to the stovetop, increasing the heat slightly. Sprinkle the scallops with salt and pepper. Add 1 tablespoon olive oil to the hot skillet and immediately arrange the scallops in a single layer in the skillet. Sear for 2 minutes on each side or until caramelized. Add the vermouth and cook for 1 to 2 minutes, stirring frequently. Spoon the scallops over the artichoke mixture and serve immediately.

Shrimp and Artichokes

Serves 4

Downtown Dunedin's waterfront would not be the same without Bon Appetit serving meals such as Shrimp and Artichokes.

Spice Blend
3½ teaspoons paprika
2 teaspoons basil
2 teaspoons thyme
2 teaspoons oregano
1½ teaspoons salt
1½ teaspoons white pepper
1½ teaspoons black pepper
1½ teaspoons cayenne pepper
1½ teaspoons garlic powder

Shrimp
2 tablespoons extra-virgin olive oil
1½ pounds (10- to 15-count) shrimp, peeled and deveined
1 pound fresh mushrooms, trimmed and sliced
1½ cups quartered artichokes
1 bunch green onions, finely sliced
3 tablespoons unsalted butter

For the spice blend, mix the paprika, basil, thyme, oregano, salt, white pepper, black pepper, cayenne pepper and garlic powder in a bowl. Store in a jar with a tight-fitting lid.

For the shrimp, heat a sauté pan until hot and add the olive oil. Heat until the oil is hot. Add the shrimp and 2 tablespoons of the Spice Blend to the hot oil and toss to coat. Cook for 2 minutes and turn the shrimp. Stir in the mushrooms and artichokes. Cook for 4 minutes longer or until the shrimp turn pink, stirring frequently; do not overcook. Stir in the green onions and butter and cook until heated through, stirring frequently. Spoon the shrimp mixture over hot cooked rice.

Barbecued Shrimp

Serves 8

2 pounds medium to large shrimp
1 tablespoon paprika
1 tablespoon garlic powder
1 tablespoon salt
1 tablespoon cayenne pepper
1 tablespoon oregano
1 tablespoon thyme
1 tablespoon olive oil
1/4 cup chopped onion
3 garlic cloves, chopped

3 bay leaves
3 lemons, peeled and cut into wedges
3 cups water
1/2 cup Worcestershire sauce
1/2 cup white wine
1 teaspoon salt
black pepper to taste
1 tablespoon olive oil
2 cups heavy cream
2 tablespoons butter

Peel and devein the shrimp, reserving the shells. Mix the paprika, garlic powder, 1 tablespoon salt, cayenne pepper, oregano and thyme in a bowl. Sprinkle the shrimp with 1/2 of the seasoning blend and chill, covered, in the refrigerator.

Heat 1 tablespoon olive oil in a large saucepan over high heat. Sauté the onion and garlic in the hot oil for 1 minute. Stir in the reserved shrimp shells, remaining seasoning blend, bay leaves, lemons, water, Worcestershire sauce, wine, 1 teaspoon salt and black pepper. Bring to a boil; reduce the heat.

Simmer for 30 minutes, stirring occasionally. Remove from the heat and let stand until cool. Strain into a saucepan, discarding the solids. The strained liquid should measure about 1 1/2 cups. Bring to a boil and boil for 20 minutes or until thick and syrupy, stirring occasionally. Remove from the heat.

Sauté the shrimp in 1 tablespoon olive oil in a skillet for 3 minutes. Add the cream and the syrupy mixture and mix well. Cook for 2 to 3 minutes, stirring frequently. Remove the shrimp to a heated bowl using a slotted spoon and reserving the sauce. Whisk the butter into the reserved sauce and serve with the shrimp.

Chef's Tip: Serve with Garlic Cheese Grits on page 28 or garlic mashed potatoes.

Oven-Barbecued Shrimp

Serves 10 to 12 as appetizer or
4 to 6 as a main entrée

6 pounds large shrimp, unpeeled
1 cup (2 sticks) unsalted butter, melted
1 cup (2 sticks) margarine, melted
6 to 8 tablespoons Worcestershire sauce
3 or 4 garlic cloves, minced

1/4 cup freshly ground pepper
juice of 2 lemons
2 teaspoons Tabasco sauce
2 teaspoons salt
1 teaspoon rosemary
2 lemons, sliced

Devein the shrimp, leaving the shells intact. Combine the next 9 ingredients in a bowl and mix well.

Pour just enough of the butter mixture into a 9×13-inch baking dish to cover the bottom. Layer the shrimp and lemons over the butter mixture and drizzle with the remaining butter mixture. Bake at 400 degrees for 15 to 20 minutes or until the shrimp turn pink. Serve with hot crusty French bread and lots of napkins.

Firecracker Shrimp

Serves 4

1 pound large white Gulf shrimp
3 tablespoons virgin olive oil
2 tablespoons chopped fresh parsley
2 teaspoons grated lemon zest

2 teaspoons chopped fresh thyme
1/4 teaspoon cayenne pepper
5 ounces pancetta, sliced
juice of 1 lemon

Peel and devein the shrimp, leaving the tails intact. Combine the olive oil, 1 tablespoon of the parsley, lemon zest, thyme and cayenne pepper in a shallow bowl and mix well. Add the shrimp and toss to coat. Marinate, covered, in the refrigerator for 2 hours, stirring occasionally; drain.

Wrap each shrimp entirely with 1 slice of the pancetta and thread onto skewers. Grill over hot coals for 2 minutes per side or until the pancetta begins to color and the shrimp turn pink. Remove the skewers and arrange the shrimp on a platter. Drizzle with the lemon juice and sprinkle with the remaining 1 tablespoon parsley. Serve immediately with risotto or mashed potatoes.

Clearwater Boil

Serves 8 to 10

2 gallons water
1 pound sausage, sliced or chopped
2 pounds small red potatoes
1 large onion, cut lengthwise
  into quarters
2 green bell peppers, cut lengthwise
  into quarters

3 ribs celery
6 tablespoons (or more) Old Bay
  seasoning, or to taste
7 ears of corn, each cut into halves
3 pounds shrimp

Bring the water to a boil in a stockpot. Add the sausage, potatoes, onion, bell peppers, celery and Old Bay seasoning and return to a boil.

Boil for 12 minutes. Add the corn and boil for 10 minutes. Stir in the shrimp and boil until the shrimp turn pink, stirring occasionally.

Strain, discarding the liquid. Arrange the sausage, potatoes, onion, bell peppers, celery, corn and shrimp on a large platter and serve immediately.

Chef's Tip: Utensils needed...none. A fun summer meal that needs lots of napkins!

Creole Jambalaya

Serves 4 to 6

2 tablespoons margarine
3/4 cup chopped onion
1/2 cup chopped celery
1/4 cup chopped green bell pepper
1 tablespoon chopped fresh parsley
1 garlic clove, minced
1 pound smoked sausage, sliced or
   chopped
2 (28-ounce) cans tomatoes, drained
   and chopped

1 (10-ounce) can beef broth
1 broth can water
1 cup long grain rice
1 teaspoon sugar
1/2 teaspoon thyme, crushed
1/2 teaspoon chili powder
1/4 teaspoon pepper
2 pounds deveined peeled shrimp

Heat the margarine in a Dutch oven until melted. Stir in the onion, celery, bell pepper, parsley and garlic. Cook, covered, until the vegetables are tender, stirring occasionally. Add the sausage, tomatoes, beef broth, water, rice, sugar, thyme, chili powder and pepper and mix well.

Simmer, covered, for 25 minutes or until the rice is tender, stirring occasionally. Stir in the shrimp. Simmer for 5 to 10 minutes longer or until the shrimp turn pink and the jambalaya is the desired consistency, stirring occasionally.

Jalapeño Grits

Serves 6

1 cup stone-ground grits
4 cups water
1 teaspoon salt
2 cups (8 ounces) shredded
   Pepper Jack cheese
1/2 cup (1 stick) butter,
   chopped

3 eggs, beaten
1 tablespoon finely chopped
   jalapeño chile
salt and pepper to taste

Most grocery stores sell quick-cooking grits. These are ground very fine and steam quickly. To prepare, use a liquid-to-dry grits proportion of four to one. Although they cook more quickly, they improve in taste and texture with longer cooking. So don't be afraid to use quick-cooking grits in the recipes included in this book.

Combine the grits with cold water to cover in a bowl. Skim off the chaff; drain. Bring 4 cups water and 1 teaspoon salt to a boil in a medium saucepan. Add the grits gradually, stirring constantly. Reduce the heat and simmer for 30 minutes or until thick and creamy, stirring frequently.

Remove from the heat. Add the cheese to the grits and mix well. Add the butter and beat until smooth. Stir in the eggs and jalapeño chile. Season with salt and pepper to taste. Spoon into a greased 2-quart baking dish. Bake at 350 degrees for 35 minutes or until the grits are firm and the top is slightly brown.

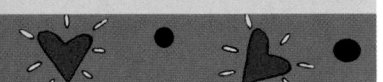

Smoked Gouda Grits

Serves 8

4 cups chicken broth
3 cups milk
2 teaspoons salt

1 1/4 cups grits
1 1/2 cups (6 ounces) shredded
   smoked Gouda cheese

Bring the chicken broth, milk and salt to a boil in a large saucepan over medium-high heat. Add the grits gradually, stirring constantly. Reduce the heat to medium-low and simmer, covered, for 20 minutes, stirring occasionally. Remove from the heat and stir in the cheese.

Southern Fried Grits

Serves 6 to 8

1 cup stone-ground grits
4 cups water
1 teaspoon salt, or to taste
1 cup (4 ounces) shredded
    sharp Cheddar cheese

2 tablespoons butter
salt and pepper to taste
1 cup flour
1/4 cup (1/2 stick) butter

Combine the grits with cold water to cover in a bowl. Skim off the chaff; drain. Bring 4 cups water and 1 teaspoon salt to a boil in a medium saucepan. Add the grits gradually, stirring constantly. Reduce the heat and simmer for 30 minutes or until thick and creamy, stirring frequently.

Remove from the heat. Add the cheese and 2 tablespoons butter and stir until smooth. Season with salt and pepper to taste. Spoon into an ungreased 5×9-inch pan. Let stand for 1 hour or until cool and firm. Invert the grits onto a work surface and cut into 1/4- to 1/2-inch slices.

Combine the flour, salt and pepper in a shallow dish. Coat all sides of the grit slices with the flour mixture. Melt 1/4 cup butter in a medium skillet over medium-high heat. Add the prepared grit slices and cook for 5 minutes or until golden brown. Turn and cook for 5 minutes longer. You may add 1/2 cup crumbled cooked sausage or 1/2 cup chopped cooked bacon to the grits before spooning into the pan to cool if desired.

Indian hominy, or dried whole corn kernels boiled with lye to loosen the husks, yielded the first English recipe for hominy grits. Now grits refers mostly to corn grits— dried corn that has been hulled and roughly ground.

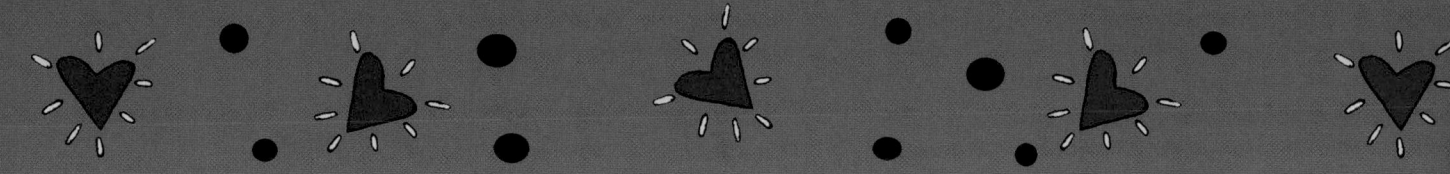

Asparagus and Basmati Rice

Serves 4 to 6

1 1/2 cups basmati rice
2 tablespoons olive oil
1/8 teaspoon saffron
1 tablespoon white pepper
2 cups water
juice of 1/2 lemon
3 pounds asparagus, trimmed

1 1/2 cups Sauterne wine
1 teaspoon sugar
1 cup (4 ounces) grated Romano cheese
1 cup (4 ounces) shredded Gruyère cheese
1/2 cup (1 stick) butter, cubed

Combine the rice, olive oil, saffron and white pepper in a skillet and sauté until the rice is golden. Combine the water and lemon juice in a large saucepan and bring to a boil. Tie the asparagus loosely with kitchen twine and place upright in a steamer basket or on a rack placed over the boiling water. Steam, covered, until tender-crisp. Drain the asparagus, reserving 1 1/2 cups of the liquid. Remove the kitchen twine.

Add the wine, sugar and reserved liquid to the rice and cook, covered, over medium-low heat for 20 minutes or until all of the liquid is absorbed. Spoon the rice evenly over the bottom of a buttered 9×9-inch baking dish. Layer the asparagus, Romano cheese, Gruyère cheese and butter half at a time over the rice. Bake, covered with foil, at 350 degrees for 15 minutes.

Butter Beans

Serves 6 to 8

3 (14-ounce) cans butter beans
1 cup sour cream
1 cup packed brown sugar

3 to 4 teaspoons dry mustard
1/4 cup (1/2 stick) butter, softened
salt and pepper to taste

Drain the beans, reserving the liquid. Combine the beans, sour cream, brown sugar, dry mustard, butter and salt and pepper in a large bowl and mix well. Spoon into a baking dish. Bake, uncovered, at 300 degrees for 3 hours, adding the reserved liquid as needed.

Southern Corn Pudding

Serves 6 to 10

1 1/8 cups milk
3 tablespoons butter
3 (11-ounce) cans white Shoe Peg
  corn, drained

3 eggs, lightly beaten
3 tablespoons sugar
1/4 teaspoon pepper

Heat the milk in a small saucepan to just below boiling, stirring frequently. Remove from the heat and add the butter, stirring until melted. Combine the milk mixture, corn, eggs, sugar and pepper in a bowl and mix well. Spoon into a 3-quart baking dish. Bake at 350 degrees for 45 to 50 minutes or until golden and bubbly.

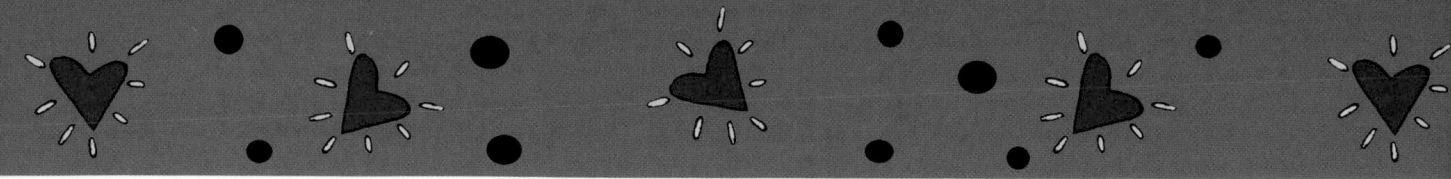

Mediterranean Lentils

Serves 4 to 6

6 cups vegetable consommé
2 cups lentils
1 large onion
1 tablespoon olive oil
3 large onions, chopped
4 garlic cloves, chopped
7 tablespoons olive oil

2 teaspoons curry powder
1/2 teaspoon red pepper
1/2 teaspoon crushed
  peppercorns
1/2 teaspoon turmeric
1 clove, crushed

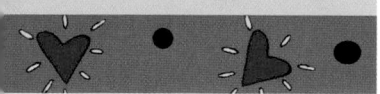

The Clearwater East-West Trail's eleven miles connects Tampa Bay to the Gulf of Mexico at Clearwater Beach. A wonderful place to jog, walk, ride, or skate, the trail joins residential and commercial areas to numerous recreational opportunities.

Bring the consommé to a gentle boil in a large saucepan over medium-high heat. Add the lentils, 1 onion and 1 tablespoon olive oil. Reduce the heat and simmer, covered, for 1 hour. Drain and discard the onion.

Cook 3 onions and the garlic in 7 tablespoons olive oil in a skillet until tender, stirring frequently. Mash the curry powder, red pepper, peppercorns, turmeric and clove with the back of a wooden spoon until combined in a small pan over medium heat. Add the spice mixture and lentils to the onion mixture and simmer for 15 minutes or until the lentils are soft but still maintain their shape, stirring occasionally.

Savory Mushroom Pie

Serves 6 to 8

2¹/2 cups chopped onions
¹/4 cup (¹/2 stick) butter
8 cups chopped assorted mushrooms
1 teaspoon thyme
¹/4 cup Marsala wine
¹/2 teaspoon salt

freshly ground pepper to taste
3 tablespoons flour
1 (2-crust) pie pastry
1 egg
1 tablespoon water

Sauté the onions in the butter in a large skillet over medium heat until soft and golden. Add the mushrooms and thyme and cook until the mushrooms release their juices and are reduced in volume, stirring frequently. Add the wine and cook until the liquid is reduced by half. Season with the salt and pepper. Sprinkle with the flour and cook until slightly thickened, stirring constantly. Remove from the heat. Let stand until cool.

Roll the pie pastry into a 14-inch circle on a lightly floured surface. Fit into a 9-inch pie plate. The pastry will hang over the edge of the pie plate. Spoon the mushroom mixture evenly into the prepared pie plate. Fold the overhanging edge of the pie pastry toward the center of the pie plate, covering the outer edge of the mushroom mixture. Whisk together the egg and water in a small bowl. Brush the mixture over the pie pastry. Bake at 400 degrees for 30 to 35 minutes or until the crust is golden. Serve warm or at room temperature.

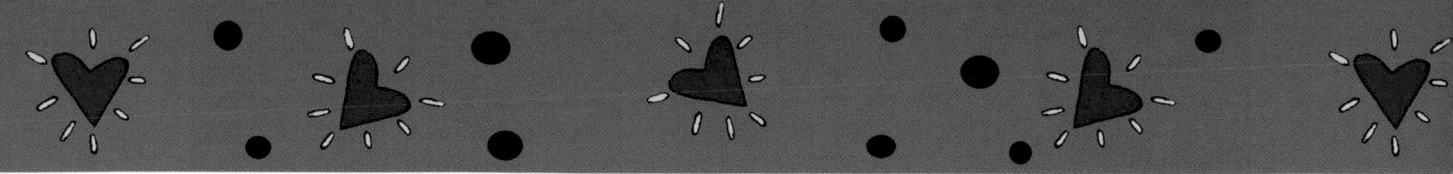

Sweet Onion Pudding

Serves 8

2 cups heavy cream
1 (3-ounce) package shredded
  Parmesan cheese
6 eggs, lightly beaten
3 tablespoons flour

2 tablespoons sugar
2 teaspoons baking powder
1 teaspoon salt
1/2 cup (1 stick) butter or margarine
6 sweet onions, thinly sliced

Combine the cream, Parmesan cheese and eggs in a large bowl and mix well. Combine the flour, sugar, baking powder and salt in a small bowl. Stir into the egg mixture gradually.

Melt the butter in a large skillet over medium heat. Add the onions and cook for 30 to 40 minutes or until caramel-colored, stirring frequently. Add the onions to the egg mixture and mix well. Spoon into a lightly greased 9×13-inch baking dish. Bake at 350 degrees for 30 minutes or until set. Serve with turkey or beef tenderloin.

Minty Roasted Potatoes

Serves 4 to 6

8 to 10 red new potatoes
1/4 cup olive oil
1 tablespoon coarse kosher salt
1 teaspoon freshly ground pepper

2 to 4 garlic cloves, finely chopped
2 tablespoons coarsely chopped fresh
  mint leaves

Pierce the potatoes with a fork and arrange on a baking sheet. Bake at 350 degrees for 1 1/2 hours. Cut the potatoes into quarters and place in a large bowl. Add the olive oil, kosher salt, pepper and garlic and toss gently to combine. Add the mint and toss gently. Serve hot or at room temperature.

Chef's Tip: For all root vegetables, including potatoes, begin the boiling process with cold water. This dish makes a fabulous side to grilled fish or Chef John Lewis' Lamb Paillarde Burger (page 89).

Sweet Potato Soufflé

Serves 8 to10

Pecan Topping
1 cup packed brown sugar
1/2 cup flour
1/2 cup (1 stick) butter, softened
1 cup pecans
1 1/2 cups coconut (optional)

Sweet Potatoes
2 1/2 pounds sweet potatoes, baked
2 eggs
1/2 cup milk
1/2 cup (1 stick) butter, softened
1 teaspoon vanilla
1 cup sugar
1/2 teaspoon salt

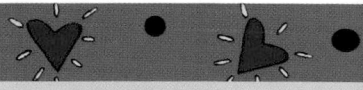

The Gulf Coast Museum of Art, located at Pinewood Cultural Village in Largo along with the Botanical Gardens and Heritage Village, features contemporary Florida art with a special focus on contemporary craft media objects from the twelve southeastern states.

For the topping, combine the brown sugar and flour in a small bowl. Cut in the butter until crumbly. Add the pecans and coconut and mix well.

For the sweet potatoes, cut the potatoes into halves, remove the pulp to a large bowl and discard the shells. Mash the pulp. Add the eggs, milk, butter, vanilla, sugar and salt and mix well. Spoon into a buttered 9×13-inch baking dish. Sprinkle with the topping. Bake at 350 degrees for 40 to 45 minutes or until golden brown.

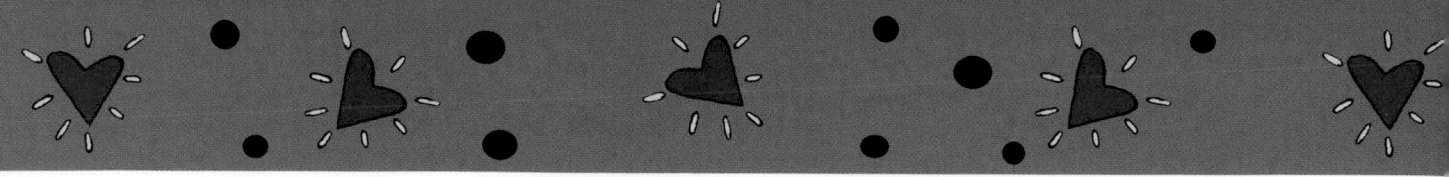

Sautéed Spinach with Raisins and Pine Nuts

Serves 4 to 6

2 pounds fresh spinach, coarsely
   chopped
2 garlic cloves, crushed
1 tablespoon olive oil

1/3 cup raisins
1/3 cup pine nuts, lightly toasted
salt and pepper to taste

Combine the spinach with boiling water to cover in a large saucepan and boil
for 10 seconds. Drain and squeeze the excess liquid from the spinach. Sauté
the garlic in the olive oil in a large skillet until golden but not brown. Remove
the garlic and discard. Add the raisins and pine nuts to the oil in the skillet and
sauté for 1 minute. Add the spinach, salt and pepper and cook over low heat
for 3 minutes, stirring constantly. Serve immediately. You may substitute dried
cranberries for the raisins if desired.

Easy Spaghetti Squash

Serves 4

1/2 cup thinly sliced celery
1/4 cup thinly sliced onion
2 garlic cloves, minced
1/4 cup (1/2 stick) butter

4 cups hot cooked spaghetti squash
3 ounces shredded Parmesan cheese
1/4 cup chopped fresh parsley
1 teaspoon oregano

Sauté the celery, onion and garlic in the butter in a nonstick skillet for 2 minutes.
Combine with the remaining ingredients in a bowl and toss gently. For a fast and
easy main dish, toss with 4 ounces chopped cooked chicken.

Chef's Tip: To microwave spaghetti squash, pierce the squash all over
with a fork. Microwave on High for 16 to 19 minutes. Remove from the
microwave and let stand for 10 minutes.

Acorn Squash Stuffed with Apple Spiced Grits

Serves 6

3 acorn squash
1 cup stone-ground grits
4 cups water
1 teaspoon salt
3 tablespoons butter, melted
2/3 cup packed brown sugar

1 teaspoon nutmeg
1/2 teaspoon cinnamon
1/2 cup chopped apple
1/4 cup chopped pecans
1/4 cup raisins

Cut the squash into halves horizontally and remove the seeds. Fill a shallow baking dish with 1 inch of water. Arrange the squash cut side down in the baking dish. Bake at 350 degrees for 30 to 45 minutes or until tender. Drain the water from the baking dish and arrange the squash cut side up in the dish. Combine the grits with cold water to cover in a bowl. Skim off the chaff; drain. Bring 4 cups water and the salt to a boil in a medium saucepan. Add the grits gradually, stirring constantly. Reduce the heat to low and simmer for 30 minutes or until thick and creamy, stirring frequently.

Combine the grits, butter, brown sugar, nutmeg, cinnamon, apple, pecans and raisins in a bowl and mix well. Spoon into the squash halves. Bake at 350 degrees for 15 minutes or until heated through.

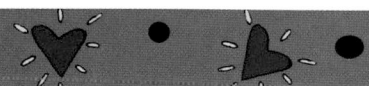

Honeymoon Island, one of the area's best eco-tourism focal points, is located across the Dunedin Causeway. It is a typical Gulf Coast barrier island with white sand beaches on the Gulf side and mangrove swamps on the bay side.

Stuffed Squash

Serves 2

1 acorn squash
olive oil
1/2 apple, peeled and
   finely chopped
1/2 teaspoon lime juice
3/4 teaspoon olive oil
1/8 teaspoon crushed red
   pepper

2 garlic cloves, minced
1/4 cup sliced scallions
1/2 cup coarsely shredded
   carrots
6 ounces bulk pork sausage
   or ground beef
1/2 cup craisins
1/8 cup cooking sherry

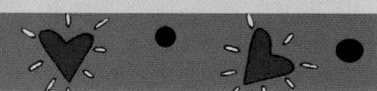

*Selected as the
SportsTown for
the state of
Florida by* Sports
Illustrated, *the city
of Clearwater offers
a wide array of
active opportunities
for elite athletes,
weekend warriors,
and out-of-town
visitors alike.*

Cut the squash in half and remove the seeds. Fill a shallow baking dish with 1 inch of water. Place the squash halves cut side down in the prepared dish. Bake at 375 degrees for 1 hour. Drain the water from the dish. Brush the peel with olive oil and place cut side up in the baking dish.

Place the apple in a bowl and drizzle with the lime juice. Heat 3/4 teaspoon olive oil and the red pepper in a 10-inch skillet over medium-high heat. Add the garlic, scallions and carrots and sauté for 3 minutes. Add the sausage and cook for 5 minutes or until brown and crumbly, stirring frequently; drain. Add the apple, craisins and sherry. Reduce the heat to low and simmer for 5 minutes, stirring occasionally. Spoon half the sausage mixture into each squash half. Bake, covered with foil, at 375 degrees for 10 minutes or until heated through.

Fried Green Tomatoes and Squash

Serves 4

1/2 cup (2 ounces) grated Parmesan cheese
salt and freshly ground pepper to taste
2 green tomatoes, thinly sliced
1 to 2 zucchini, thinly sliced
2 to 3 yellow squash, thinly sliced
1/2 cup (2 ounces) grated Parmesan cheese

Warm a nonstick skillet over medium-low heat. Combine 1/2 cup Parmesan cheese, salt and pepper in a resealable plastic bag and shake to mix. Add the tomatoes and shake to coat well. Spray the skillet with olive oil cooking spray. Arrange the tomato slices in the prepared skillet and cook for 3 minutes on each side or until golden brown. Remove to a paper towel to drain. Place the zucchini and yellow squash in a colander and rinse with water. Shake the colander to remove excess water. Toss the zucchini and yellow squash with 1/2 cup Parmesan cheese in a bowl. Spray the skillet with additional olive oil cooking spray. Add the zucchini and yellow squash and sauté until tender-crisp. Arrange on a serving platter with the prepared tomatoes and serve immediately.

Hint: This is a healthy alternative to the traditional fried green tomatoes and is equally as flavorful.

Oven-Roasted Tomatoes

Serves 12

6 tomatoes, halved
12 basil leaves
3 garlic cloves, thinly sliced
6 thyme leaves, chopped
3 tablespoons olive oil

3 tablespoons balsamic
vinegar
pepper to taste
kosher salt to taste

Designated as a Blue Wave Beach, Clearwater was acknowledged by the Clean Beaches Council. This organization promotes beaches that are managed to protect their natural assets, ensuring excellence in the areas of water quality, cleanliness, safety, services, habitat conservation, information, education, and erosion management.

Arrange the tomatoes in a shallow baking pan. Top each with a basil leaf. Sprinkle with the garlic and thyme. Drizzle with the olive oil and balsamic vinegar. Marinate, covered, in the refrigerator for 8 hours.

Bake at 225 degrees for 2 1/2 hours or until the tomatoes are reduced by half. Remove from the oven and let stand until cool. Remove the peel from the tomatoes. The tomatoes may be stored for up to 1 week in the refrigerator.

Reserve the seasoned olive oil mixture for another use. The garlic may be mashed and spread over meat or fish. Drizzle olive oil over meat or fish before cooking.

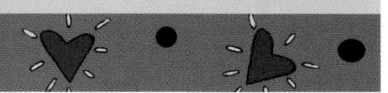

Basil-Marinated Grilled Vegetables

Serves 4

Basil Marinade

1/4 cup seasoned rice vinegar
1/4 cup extra-virgin olive oil
2 teaspoons freshly ground pepper
1/2 teaspoon salt
1/2 cup lightly packed fresh
  basil leaves
basil sprigs
1/3 cup shaved Parmesan cheese

Vegetables

1/2 to 1 pound whole mushrooms
1 (1-pint) package cherry tomatoes
1 to 2 green bell peppers
2 Vidalia onions, cut into eighths
1 bunch asparagus, trimmed

For the marinade, combine the vinegar, olive oil, pepper, salt, basil leaves, basil sprigs and Parmesan cheese in a large resealable plastic bag and shake to combine.

For the vegetables, chop the mushrooms, bell peppers, onions and asparagus into equal-size pieces. Place the vegetables and cherry tomatoes in the bag with the marinade and marinate at room temperature for 1 to 2 hours or in the refrigerator for 1 to 2 days, shaking occasionally; drain and discard the marinade.

Place the vegetables in a grilling basket. Grill over medium coals until tender, turning occasionally. You may thread the vegetables onto bamboo skewers that have been soaked in water instead of using a grilling basket if desired.

Chef's Tip: Vegetables take longer to grill than steaks and chicken, so be sure to put them on the grill before your meat if grilling both!

from the
Bakery

Chocolate-Crusted Amaretto Cheesecake

Serves 12

Chocolate Almond Crust
1¼ cups chocolate wafer crumbs
½ cup ground blanched almonds
6 tablespoons butter, melted
¼ teaspoon almond extract

Amaretto Filling
24 ounces cream cheese, softened
1 cup sugar
1 cup sour cream
½ teaspoon vanilla extract
½ teaspoon almond extract
3 eggs
¼ cup amaretto

For the crust, coat the side of a springform pan with butter. Combine the chocolate wafer crumbs, almonds, butter and flavoring in a bowl and mix well. Pat the crumb mixture over the bottom and up the side of the prepared pan.

For the filling, beat the cream cheese, sugar, sour cream and flavorings in a mixing bowl until blended, scraping the bowl occasionally. Add the eggs and beat at medium speed for 3 minutes. Add the liqueur and beat for 1 minute longer.

Spoon the filling into the prepared pan and bake at 350 degrees for 1 hour. Turn off the oven and let the cheesecake stand in the oven with the door closed until cool. Chill, covered, for 8 to 10 hours before serving. Garnish each serving with whipped cream and toasted sliced almonds.

Chef's Tip: The flavor of the cheesecake is enhanced if chilled for eight to ten hours before serving.

Hazelnut Raspberry Cheesecake

Serves 12

Hazelnut Crust
1 cup hazelnuts, finely ground
1 cup flour
1/4 cup packed brown sugar
1/2 cup (1 stick) butter, softened

Cream Cheese Filling
24 ounces cream cheese, softened
1 cup sugar
4 eggs, at room temperature
1 teaspoon vanilla extract

Toppings
1 cup sour cream
2 tablespoons sugar
1/2 teaspoon vanilla extract
1 pint fresh raspberries
3/4 cup raspberry preserves
2 tablespoons raspberry liqueur
  or water

For the crust, combine the hazelnuts, flour and brown sugar in a bowl and mix well. Add the butter and stir until combined. Pat over the bottom of a 10-inch springform pan. Bake at 400 degrees for 10 to 15 minutes or until light brown. Reduce the oven temperature to 350 degrees.

For the filling, combine the cream cheese, sugar, eggs and vanilla in a mixing bowl and beat at high speed for 5 minutes or until smooth, scraping the bowl occasionally. Spoon the filling over the baked crust and bake for 40 minutes or until set. Cool in the pan on a wire rack for 10 minutes. Maintain the oven temperature.

For the toppings, combine the sour cream, sugar and vanilla in a bowl and mix well. Spread the sour cream mixture over the top of the cheesecake. Bake for 5 minutes. Cool in the pan on a wire rack.

Arrange the raspberries in circles over the top of the cheesecake, starting from the middle. Combine the preserves and liqueur in a small saucepan and mix well. Simmer until the preserves melt, stirring occasionally. Drizzle the preserves mixture over the top of the cheesecake and chill, covered, until serving time.

Raspberry Swirl

Serves 12

Chocolate Crust

1³/4 cups chocolate wafer crumbs
3 tablespoons butter, melted
2 tablespoons sugar
¹/4 teaspoon almond extract

Raspberry Filling and Assembly

8 ounces cream cheese, softened
1 cup sugar
12 ounces frozen whipped topping,
    thawed
1 (10-ounce) package frozen
    raspberries, thawed

For the crust, combine the chocolate wafer crumbs, butter, sugar and flavoring in a bowl and mix well. Pat the crumb mixture over the bottom of a springform pan. Bake at 375 degrees for 10 minutes.

For the filling, beat the cream cheese and sugar in a mixing bowl until creamy, scraping the bowl occasionally. Add the whipped topping and beat until blended. Process the raspberries in a blender until puréed. Fold ¹/2 of the raspberry purée into the cream cheese mixture and spread over the baked layer.

Swirl the remaining purée into the cream cheese layer using a knife. Freeze, covered, for 8 to 10 hours. Let stand at room temperature for 5 minutes. Garnish each serving with fresh raspberries, a sprig of mint and chocolate shavings.

Almond Tart

Serves 8

3/4 cup (1 1/2 sticks) butter,
   melted
1 1/2 cups sugar
2 eggs
1 1/3 cups flour

1 tablespoon (or more)
   almond extract
sugar to taste
1 package slivered almonds

Line a cast-iron skillet with foil and grease the foil. Combine the butter and 1 1/2 cups sugar in a mixing bowl and beat until blended. Add the eggs 1 at a time, beating well after each addition. Stir in the flour and flavoring.

Spoon the batter into the prepared skillet and sprinkle with sugar to taste and the almonds. Bake at 350 degrees for 30 minutes. Immediately remove the tart from the skillet and let stand in the foil until cool. Slice as desired and serve with ice cream, whipped cream and/or berries.

When Pinellas County Schools embarked on the exciting adventure of implementing School Choice programs, the Junior League of Clearwater-Dunedin stepped up with a signature project called F.U.N. Bus, a program designed to supplement cultural and science field trips by providing the availability to more than 113,000 students to attend out-of-class experiences.

Apple Delight

Serves 6 to 8

1 cup flour
2 tablespoons sugar
1/4 teaspoon grated nutmeg
1 3/4 cups milk
6 eggs
1/4 cup (1/2 stick) butter,
   melted
2 teaspoons vanilla extract

1/4 cup packed brown sugar
1 teaspoon cinnamon
1/4 teaspoon grated nutmeg
3 tablespoons butter
2 large Red Delicious apples,
   thinly sliced
1/2 cup packed brown sugar

*The arts come alive
outside! Shakespeare
in the Park brings
the bard to life in
downtown St.
Petersburg, while
numerous artists
are drawn to the
beautiful waterfront
setting of Coachman
Park in downtown
Clearwater.*

Combine the flour, sugar and 1/4 teaspoon nutmeg in a bowl and mix well. Add the milk, eggs, 1/4 cup melted butter and vanilla and whisk until blended. Let stand for 30 minutes. Combine 1/4 cup brown sugar, cinnamon and 1/4 teaspoon nutmeg in a small bowl. Sprinkle over the batter.

Heat 3 tablespoons butter in a 10-inch ovenproof skillet over medium heat. Brush the sides and bottom with the melted butter. Arrange the apples over the bottom of the prepared skillet. Sprinkle the apples with 1/2 cup brown sugar. Increase the heat to medium-high and cook until the mixture bubbles, stirring occasionally. Pour the batter over the apples. Bake at 425 degrees for 15 minutes. Reduce the oven temperature to 375 degrees and bake for 12 minutes. Serve warm with vanilla ice cream.

Godiva Chocolate Mousse

Serves 6

Compliments of Bon Appetit Restaurant

6 ounces semisweet chocolate,
   melted
1/4 cup (1/2 stick) butter, melted
   and warm
1/2 cup sugar

4 egg yolks
4 egg whites
1 cup whipping cream
2 tablespoons Godiva liqueur

Blend the chocolate and butter in a bowl. Beat 1/4 cup of the sugar and the egg yolks in a mixing bowl until the volume has doubled and the mixture is light and creamy. Beat the egg whites in a mixing bowl until soft peaks form. Add the remaining 1/4 cup sugar to the egg whites gradually, beating constantly until stiff peaks form. Fold the egg whites into the egg yolk mixture and then fold in the chocolate mixture. Beat the whipping cream in a mixing bowl until stiff peaks form and fold into the chocolate mixture. Fold in the liqueur. Chill, covered, until serving time. To serve, spoon or pipe the mousse into stemmed dessert dishes.

Tropical Delight

Serves 12

1 1/4 cups graham cracker crumbs
1/2 cup (1 stick) butter, melted
2 cups sifted confectioners' sugar
1/2 cup (1 stick) butter
2 pasteurized eggs
3 or 4 bananas, sliced

1 (20-ounce) can crushed
   pineapple, drained
16 ounces fresh or drained frozen
   strawberries
frozen whipped topping, thawed

Combine the graham cracker crumbs and melted butter in a bowl and mix well. Pat the crumb mixture over the bottom of a 7×11-inch dish. Beat the confectioners' sugar, butter and eggs in a mixing bowl until light and fluffy, scraping the bowl occasionally. Spread over the crumb layer.

Layer the bananas, pineapple and strawberries over the prepared layers and spread with whipped topping. Chill, covered, for 3 to 4 hours before serving.

Pastry Swans with Grand Marnier Cream

Serves 8

Pastry
1 cup water
1/2 cup (1 stick) butter
1/4 teaspoon salt
1 cup flour
4 eggs, lightly beaten

Grand Marnier Cream and Assembly
2 cups whipping cream
2 tablespoons (or more) confectioners' sugar
2 tablespoons Grand Marnier confectioners' sugar to taste

The Suncoast Seabird Sanctuary is home to more than 600 birds that represent dozens of species, living and recuperating in the sanctuary. The center breeds permanently disabled birds in hopes of releasing their offspring back into nature. The sanctuary treats over 10,000 injured birds annually.

For the pastry, bring the water, butter and salt to a boil in a saucepan and boil until the butter melts. Reduce the heat to low and stir in the flour with a wooden spoon. Cook until the mixture forms a ball, stirring frequently. Remove from the heat. Add the eggs and beat until blended.

Reserve 1/2 cup of the batter. Drop the remaining batter into 8 large mounds on a greased baking sheet, swirling the top of each mound; these will be the swan's bodies. Pipe the reserved batter into 8 candy cane shapes on the baking sheet to represent the swan's necks. Bake the swan necks at 375 degrees for 25 to 30 minutes and remove to a wire rack to cool. Bake the swan bodies for 50 minutes or until golden brown. Cut a slit in the side of each and bake for 10 minutes longer. Remove to a wire rack to cool.

For the cream, beat the whipping cream in a mixing bowl until soft peaks form. Add 2 tablespoons confectioners' sugar and the liqueur and mix well. Fill the swan bodies with the filling and attach the swan necks. Dust each swan with confectioners' sugar to taste and chill until serving time.

Margarita Ice Cream Torte

Serves 12

30 chocolate sandwich cookies
1/4 cup (1/2 stick) butter, melted
1/2 cup frozen lemonade concentrate, thawed
1/4 cup plus 2 tablespoons Tequila
2 tablespoons plus 2 teaspoons fresh lime juice
2 tablespoons Triple Sec
1 teaspoon grated lime zest
5 drops of green food coloring
2 quarts vanilla ice cream, softened

Process the cookies in a food processor until crumbled. Add the butter and process until coarsely ground. Reserve 2 tablespoons of the crumb mixture. Pat the remaining crumb mixture over the bottom of a 9-inch springform pan and bake at 350 degrees for 10 minutes. Cool in the pan on a wire rack.

Combine the lemonade concentrate, Tequila, lime juice, Triple Sec, lime zest and food coloring in a bowl and mix well. Add the ice cream and stir until blended. Spread the ice cream mixture over the prepared layer and sprinkle with the reserved crumbs. Freeze, covered, for 8 to 10 hours. Remove the side of the pan and slice. Garnish with lime slices and whipped cream and serve immediately.

Decadent Chocolate Torte

Serves 12 to 15

Brownie Layer

2 ounces unsweetened chocolate
1/4 cup (1/2 stick) butter
1 cup sugar
2 egg yolks
1/4 cup milk
1 teaspoon vanilla extract
3/4 cup flour
1/2 teaspoon baking powder
1/4 teaspoon salt
2 egg whites
1 cup macadamia nuts or any nut,
   coarsely chopped

Truffle Layer

2 cups (12 ounces) semisweet
   chocolate chips
3/4 cup sugar
1/4 cup water
1 envelope unflavored gelatin
1 1/4 cups (2 1/2 sticks) butter
1 tablespoon instant espresso
   coffee powder
5 egg yolks
3 tablespoons Grand Marnier or
   any brandy

Mousse Layer and Assembly

1 package Pepperidge Farm® Pirouline
   Chocolate Wafer Rolls
1 cup whipping cream

For the brownie layer, heat the chocolate in a double boiler over hot water until melted, stirring occasionally. Remove from the heat and let stand until cool. Beat the butter in a mixing bowl until creamy. Add the sugar gradually, beating constantly until light and fluffy. Beat in the chocolate until blended. Add the egg yolks 1 at a time, beating well after each addition. Add the milk and vanilla and beat until smooth.

Mix the flour, baking powder and salt in a bowl and stir into the chocolate mixture. Beat the egg whites in a mixing bowl until soft peaks form and fold into the chocolate mixture with a rubber spatula. Stir in the macadamia nuts. Spoon the batter into a greased and floured 9 1/2- or 10-inch springform pan. Bake at 350 degrees for 35 minutes. Cool in the pan on a wire rack.

For the truffle layer, process the chocolate chips and sugar in a food processor until finely ground. Pour the water into a heavy 2-quart saucepan and sprinkle the gelatin over the top. Let stand for 2 minutes to soften. Add the butter and espresso powder and bring to a boil, stirring frequently.

Add the boiling butter mixture to the chocolate chip mixture, processing constantly until the chocolate chips melt. Add the egg yolks 1 at a time, processing until blended after each addition. Add the liqueur and process until smooth. Return the chocolate mixture to the saucepan and cook over medium-high heat for 6 to 7 minutes or until thickened, stirring frequently.

Pour into a large bowl and place the bowl in a larger container filled with ice and water. Let stand until chilled, scraping the side of the bowl and stirring frequently. The mixture will become even thicker. Spread 1/2 of the cooled chocolate mixture over the top of the baked layer, reserving the remaining chocolate mixture for the mousse layer. You may substitute 1/4 cup strong coffee for the water and espresso powder.

For the mousse layer, cut the cookies into halves and insert cut side down around the edge of the springform pan, pushing down just to the brownie layer. If these cookies are not available, use any other cookie that would make an attractive border. Beat the whipping cream in a mixing bowl until stiff peaks form. Fold the reserved chocolate mixture into the whipped cream until white streaks no longer appear and spread over the prepared layers. Chill, covered, until serving time.

Slice as desired and garnish each serving with a chocolate-covered strawberry. You may add just 1/4 of the reserved chocolate mixture to the whipped cream and spoon the remaining chocolate mixture into a pastry bag fitted with a small tip and pipe in a decorative pattern over the top of the torte.

Caramel Flan

Serves 6

Compliments of the Columbia Restaurant

Caramelized Sugar Topping
1 cup sugar
1 tablespoon water

Custard
1 cup sweetened condensed milk
1 cup evaporated milk
3/4 cup whole milk
3 eggs
1 1/4 teaspoons vanilla extract

For the topping, combine the sugar and water in a saucepan. Cook over medium heat until the sugar is golden brown in color, stirring constantly. Pour evenly into 6 ovenproof custard cups.

For the custard, combine the condensed milk, evaporated milk, whole milk, eggs and vanilla in a bowl and whisk until blended. Pour evenly into the prepared custard cups. Arrange the custard cups in a large baking pan and pour enough hot water into the baking pan to reach halfway up the sides of the cups. Bake at 400 degrees for 40 minutes; do not allow the water to boil. Remove the custard cups from the baking pan and chill in the refrigerator.

To serve, unmold by pressing the edges of the custards with a spoon to break away from the cup. Invert onto dessert plates. Spoon the remaining caramelized sugar from each cup over the tops of the custards.

Mocha Meringue

Serves 6 to 8

Chocolate Sauce

6 tablespoons light cream
2 ounces unsweetened chocolate
1/2 cup sugar
1/8 teaspoon salt
3 tablespoons butter
1 teaspoon vanilla extract

Meringue and Assembly

4 egg whites
1/2 teaspoon cream of tartar
1/4 teaspoon salt
1 cup sugar
1 teaspoon vanilla extract
4 cups coffee ice cream or flavor of choice, softened
1/2 cup sliced almonds, toasted

For the sauce, heat the cream and chocolate in a saucepan over low heat until blended, stirring frequently. Stir in the sugar and salt and cook until the sugar dissolves, stirring frequently. Remove from the heat. Add the butter and vanilla and stir until cool. Makes 1 cup sauce.

For the meringue, beat the egg whites, cream of tartar and salt in a mixing bowl until frothy. Add the sugar gradually, beating constantly until stiff peaks form. Add the vanilla and beat for 1 minute. Drop by spoonfuls into mounds onto a baking sheet lined with baking parchment paper to form 9 kisses. Grease a 9-inch pie plate and spread the remaining meringue over the bottom and up the side to form a shell. Bake at 300 degrees for 50 to 60 minutes or until the meringue is dry. Let stand until cool. Bake the kisses for 25 minutes or until light brown. Let stand until cool.

Layer the ice cream, almonds and 1/2 cup of the sauce 1/2 at a time over the meringue shell. Place 1 of the meringue kisses in the center and arrange the remaining kisses around the outer edge of the pie plate. Drizzle with the remaining 1/2 cup sauce and freeze until firm.

 **Heart-Healthy Tip:** If you bake at home using unsaturated oils and substituting egg whites for whole eggs, you can at least control the fat.

Chocolate Trifle

Serves 16

3 cups heavy cream
3 cups milk
3 (4-ounce) packages vanilla instant pudding mix
1 jar hot fudge ice cream topping
1/4 cup coffee liqueur

1 (16-ounce) pound cake, cut into 1-inch cubes
6 Heath candy bars, crushed
2 or 3 bananas, sliced
12 ounces frozen whipped topping, thawed
chocolate shavings or curls

Combine the cream, milk and pudding mix in a bowl and mix well. Chill until thickened. Microwave the ice cream topping for 20 seconds and mix with the liqueur in a bowl.

Layer the cake cubes, ice cream topping mixture, crushed candy bars and pudding mixture 1/2 at a time in a trifle bowl. Top with the bananas. Spread enough of the whipped topping over the top to measure 1 inch. Sprinkle with chocolate shavings or curls and chill until serving time.

158

Strawberry Trifle

Serves 10 to 12

Compliments of Bon Appetit Restaurant

8 ounces cream cheese, softened	1/2 cup raspberry purée or jam
8 ounces ricotta cheese	1 (16-ounce) yellow sponge cake, cubed
2 tablespoons lemon juice	1 cup whipped cream
2 tablespoons sugar	fresh mint leaves
2 pints fresh strawberries, cut into halves	

Beat the cream cheese, ricotta cheese, lemon juice and sugar in a mixing bowl until creamy, scraping the bowl occasionally. Toss 1 1/2 pints of the strawberries with the purée in a bowl.

Layer 1/2 of the cream cheese mixture, 1/2 of the strawberry mixture and the cake cubes in parfait glasses. Top with the remaining cream cheese mixture and remaining strawberry mixture and chill for 2 hours or longer. Top with the whipped cream, remaining 1/2 pint sliced strawberries and mint leaves just before serving.

Dunedin's village-like downtown, with its restored Main Street area, was recently named one of the "Five Most Walkable Downtowns" in America by Walking Magazine. Four miles of the Pinellas Trail winds through the downtown area.

Carrot Cake with Cream Cheese Frosting

Serves 12

Cake

2 cups flour
2 cups sugar
2 teaspoons baking soda
2 teaspoons cinnamon
1 teaspoon salt
4 eggs
1 cup vegetable oil
4 cups grated carrots
   (about 1 pound)
3/4 cup chopped nuts

Cream Cheese Frosting

8 ounces cream cheese,
   softened
2 tablespoons butter
3 1/2 cups confectioners'
   sugar, sifted
2 teaspoons milk
1/2 teaspoon vanilla extract

Two hundred nationally acclaimed artists and 50,000 attendees gather each fall to celebrate Art Harvest in Dunedin, one of the Southeast's largest fine art festivals.

For the cake, mix the flour, sugar, baking soda, cinnamon and salt in a bowl. Beat the eggs in a mixing bowl until frothy. Add the oil and beat until blended. Add the flour mixture to the egg mixture gradually, beating constantly until smooth. Stir in the carrots and nuts.

Spoon the batter evenly into 3 greased and floured 9-inch cake pans. Bake at 350 degrees for 25 minutes or until the layers test done. Cool in the pans for 10 minutes. Remove to a wire rack to cool completely.

For the frosting, beat the cream cheese and butter in a mixing bowl until creamy. Add the confectioners' sugar and milk alternately, beating well after each addition. Beat in the vanilla. Spread the frosting between the layers and over the top and side of the cake.

Chocolate Cake with Chocolate Praline Sauce

Serves 15

Compliments of Chef Mark Carey, Backwater's on Sand Key

Cake

3 cups flour
2¹/₂ cups sugar
1 cup baking cocoa
2 teaspoons baking soda
1 teaspoon baking powder
2 cups boiling water
1 cup butter-flavor oil or vegetable oil
6 eggs

Chocolate Praline Sauce

2 cups (4 sticks) butter
1 (16-ounce) package brown sugar
2 cups (12 ounces) chocolate chips
2 cups pecan pieces
1 cup water

For the cake, mix the flour, sugar, baking cocoa, baking soda and baking powder in a mixing bowl. Add the boiling water, oil and eggs and beat for 30 seconds. Spoon the batter into a greased 9×13-inch cake pan. Bake at 350 degrees for 28 minutes or until a wooden pick inserted in the center comes out clean.

For the sauce, combine the butter, brown sugar, chocolate chips, pecans and water in a saucepan. Cook over medium heat until the brown sugar dissolves and the mixture is of a sauce consistency, stirring frequently. Pour the hot sauce over the hot cake. Garnish individual dessert plates with any extra sauce.

Pound Cake with Papaya Conserve

Papaya Conserve

1/2 cup sugar
1/3 cup water
3 cups chopped ripe papaya
2 tablespoons lime juice

Pound Cake

3 cups cake flour, sifted
1/2 teaspoon baking powder
1/4 teaspoon salt
2 1/2 cups sugar
1 cup (2 sticks) butter
1/2 cup shortening
4 eggs
1 cup fruit juice
1 teaspoon lemon extract
1 teaspoon vanilla extract

For the conserve, combine the sugar and water in a heavy saucepan. Cook over medium heat for 15 minutes or until the sugar dissolves and the mixture thickens, stirring frequently. Stir in the papaya and lime juice and simmer for 20 minutes or until the mixture is reduced by 1/2, stirring frequently. Remove from the heat and cover to keep warm. Makes about 1 1/2 cups.

For the cake, mix the cake flour, baking powder and salt together. Beat the sugar, butter and shortening in a mixing bowl until creamy, scraping the bowl occasionally. Add the eggs 1 at a time, beating well after each addition. Add the flour mixture, juice and flavorings and beat until smooth. Spoon the batter into a 10-inch tube pan and bake at 325 degrees for 70 minutes; do not peek. Cool in the pan for 10 minutes. Remove to a wire rack to cool completely. Spoon the warm conserve over the cake.

 **Chef's Tip:** Prepare the Papaya Conserve in advance and store, covered, in the refrigerator. Reheat before serving.

Raspberry Lemon Cake

Serves 12

Cake
3 cups sifted cake flour
2 1/2 teaspoons baking powder
1/2 teaspoon salt
1 cup shortening
2 cups sugar
4 eggs
1 cup milk
1 teaspoon almond extract
1 teaspoon vanilla extract

Lemon Buttercream Frosting and Assembly
1 1/4 cups (2 1/2 sticks) butter, softened
3 tablespoons lemon juice
2 teaspoons grated lemon zest
3 cups sifted confectioners' sugar
1 (10-ounce) jar seedless raspberry preserves
1 pint fresh raspberries

For the cake, grease three 9-inch cake pans and line the bottoms with waxed paper. Grease and flour the waxed paper. Mix the cake flour, baking powder and salt together. Beat the shortening in a mixing bowl at medium speed until creamy. Add the sugar gradually, beating constantly until blended. Add the eggs 1 at a time, beating well after each addition. Add the cake flour mixture alternately with the milk, beginning and ending with the flour mixture and beating well after each addition. Stir in the flavorings.

Spoon the batter evenly into the prepared cake pans. Bake at 375 degrees for 18 to 20 minutes or until a wooden pick inserted in the centers comes out clean. Cool in the pans on a wire rack for 10 minutes. Remove to a wire rack to cool completely.

For the frosting, beat the butter, lemon juice and lemon zest in a mixing bowl at medium speed until creamy. Add the confectioners' sugar gradually, beating constantly until of a spreading consistency.

To serve, slice each cake layer horizontally into halves. Arrange 1 layer cut side up on a cake plate and spread with 3 tablespoons of the preserves. Repeat this process with the remaining 5 layers, omitting the preserves on the top layer.

Reserve 1 cup of the frosting and spread the remaining frosting over the top and side of the cake. Spoon the reserved frosting into a pastry bag fitted with a star tip. Pipe the frosting in a decorative pattern over the top of the cake and top with fresh raspberries. Store, covered, in the refrigerator. Use fishing line to evenly slice thin cake layers.

Key Lime Curd and Fresh Fruit Tart

Serves 8 to 12

Compliments of Chef John Lewis, La Maison Gourmet

Butter Pastry

¹/₂ cup (1 stick) butter
1 cup flour
2 tablespoons sugar
1 tablespoon vanilla extract
1 teaspoon salt

Key Lime Curd and Assembly

¹/₂ cup sugar
2 eggs
¹/₃ cup Key lime juice
grated zest of ¹/₂ Key lime
2 tablespoons unsalted butter, sliced
1 pint large strawberries, hulled, or
    1 pint fresh blueberries
¹/₂ cup apple jelly

For the pastry, heat the butter in a saucepan until melted. Combine the flour, sugar, vanilla and salt in a bowl and mix well. Add the butter and mix until the mixture forms a ball. Press over the bottom and up the side of a 9-inch tart pan and prick with a fork. Bake at 375 degrees for 15 to 18 minutes or until golden brown. Cool on a wire rack. You may substitute a commercially prepared refrigerator pie pastry for the homemade crust.

For the curd, combine the sugar and eggs in a bowl and whisk rapidly until fluffy. Add the lime juice and lime zest gradually, whisking constantly until incorporated. Pour the lime juice mixture into a double boiler and cook over boiling water for 5 to 10 minutes or until very thick, whisking constantly. Remove from the heat and whisk in the butter 1 slice at a time. Pour the curd into a bowl and cover with plastic wrap. Chill for 1 to 10 hours.

Spoon the curd into the prepared tart pan and top with the strawberries large end down. Heat the jelly in a small saucepan over medium heat until warm, stirring occasionally. Brush the jelly over the tops of the strawberries using a pastry brush. This will give the finished tart a sheen, just like commercially prepared bakery products. Chill, covered, until serving time.

Lemon Tart with Blueberries

Serve 6 to 8

Pastry

1¹/₂ cups flour
2 tablespoons sugar
¹/₈ teaspoon salt
¹/₂ cup (1 stick) unsalted butter,
   chilled and cut into chunks
1 egg yolk
2 tablespoons ice water
1 egg white, lightly beaten

Blueberry Lemon Filling

1¹/₂ cups sugar
1 cup fresh lemon juice
   (5 or 6 lemons)
¹/₄ cup heavy cream
4 eggs
Grated zest of 1 lemon
1 pint blueberries

For the pastry, combine the flour, sugar and salt in a food processor and pulse until mixed. Add the butter 1 chunk at a time and pulse until crumbly. Add the egg yolk and ice water and pulse just until combined; do not overprocess. Shape the pastry into a ball and wrap with plastic wrap. Chill for 30 minutes.

Roll the pastry into a 12-inch circle on a lightly floured surface. Fit into a 10-inch tart pan with a removable bottom and trim the edge. Arrange the tart pan on a baking sheet and bake at 350 degrees for 20 minutes. Brush with the egg white and bake for 10 minutes longer. Maintain the oven temperature.

For the filling, whisk the sugar, lemon juice, cream, eggs and lemon zest in a bowl. Stir in the blueberries. Pour into the baked shell. Bake for 25 minutes or until the center jiggles slightly.

Pecan Tarts

Pastry
6 ounces cream cheese, softened
1 cup (2 sticks) butter, softened
2 cups flour

Filling and Assembly
1 (16-ounce) package brown sugar
3 eggs, lightly beaten
1 teaspoon vanilla extract
1½ cups chopped pecans

For the pastry, beat the cream cheese, butter and flour in a mixing bowl until blended. Shape the pastry into 1-inch balls and chill, covered, in the refrigerator. Press the pastry balls over the bottoms and up the sides of miniature muffin cups.

For the filling, combine the brown sugar, eggs and vanilla in a bowl and mix well. Spoon 1½ teaspoons of the filling into each pastry-lined muffin cup and sprinkle with the pecans. Bake at 350 degrees for 25 to 30 minutes or until light brown. Remove to a wire rack to cool.

Chef's Tip: Be sure to shape the pastry into 1-inch balls prior to chilling. To properly measure flour, spoon loose flour into a measuring cup and scrape off the excess with a straight edge run across the top surface of the cup.

Chocolate Pecan Pie

Serve 8 to 10

1 recipe No-Fail Pie Pastry
(sidebar)
2 eggs
1 cup sugar
1/2 cup (1 stick) butter or
margarine, melted

1 teaspoon vanilla extract
1/4 cup cornstarch
1 cup finely chopped pecans
1 cup (6 ounces) semisweet
chocolate chips
whipped cream

Roll the pastry into a 12-inch circle on a lightly floured surface. Fit into a pie plate, trimming the edge and fluting. Beat the eggs in a mixing bowl just until combined. Add the sugar gradually, beating constantly. Add the butter and vanilla, beating well after each addition. Beat in the cornstarch. Stir in the pecans and chocolate chips.

Spoon the pecan mixture into the pastry-lined pie plate. Bake at 350 degrees for 45 to 50 minutes. Cool on a wire rack for 1 hour. Serve with whipped cream.

 **Chef's Tip:** To make your own whipped cream, beat 1/4 cup whipping cream with 2 teaspoons confectioners' sugar in a bowl. Add 1/4 teaspoon vanilla and beat until stiff peaks form.

No-Fail Pie Pastry

Cut 1/3 cup shortening into 1 cup flour until crumbly. Stir in 1/2 teaspoon salt. Add 3 tablespoons cold water 1 tablespoon at a time and mix until a soft dough forms. Shape the pastry into a ball and wrap with plastic wrap. Chill or freeze for future use. Makes 1 (9-inch) pie crust.

Black Bottom Ice Cream Pie

Serves 8

1/4 cup chocolate wafer crumbs
1/4 cup (1/2 stick) butter, melted
2 pints chocolate ice cream, slightly softened
2 ounces semisweet chocolate, melted

1 cup whipping cream
1/4 cup sugar
2 tablespoons rum or rum extract
chocolate curls

Combine the wafer crumbs and butter in a bowl and mix well. Press the crumb mixture over the bottom and up the side of a 9-inch pie plate. Freeze until firm.

Beat the ice cream in a mixing bowl at medium speed just until smooth. Add the chocolate gradually, beating constantly until blended. Spoon the ice cream mixture into the prepared pie plate and freeze until firm.

Beat the whipping cream in a mixing bowl until soft peaks form. Add the sugar and mix well. Fold in the rum. Freeze for 2 hours or until the whipped cream mixture will mound. Spoon the topping over the top of the pie and swirl. Freeze until firm and sprinkle with chocolate curls.

Coconut Rum Pecan Pie

Serves 8

2 cups pecan halves
1 unbaked (10-inch) deep-dish pie shell
1 cup sugar
1 tablespoon flour

1 cup dark corn syrup
1/2 cup (1 stick) butter, melted
3 eggs, lightly beaten
1 teaspoon vanilla extract
1/4 cup coconut rum

Spread the pecans over the bottom of the pie shell. Combine the sugar and flour in a bowl and mix well. Add the corn syrup, butter, eggs and vanilla and whisk until blended. Pour the syrup mixture over the pecans.

Bake at 375 degrees for 15 minutes. Reduce the oven temperature to 325 degrees and bake for 30 minutes longer. Brush the top of the warm pie with the rum. Cool on a wire rack.

Key Lime Pie with Macadamia Nut Crust

Serves 8

Macadamia Nut Crust

1/2 cup roasted macadamia nuts,
   rinsed and patted dry
1 cup fine vanilla wafer crumbs
   (about 26 cookies)
1/4 cup (1/2 stick) butter, melted
1 tablespoon sugar

Key Lime Filling

1 teaspoon unflavored gelatin
2 tablespoons Key lime juice
1 (14-ounce) can sweetened
   condensed milk
3 egg yolks
1/2 cup Key lime juice
1 teaspoon grated Key lime zest
1 cup chilled whipping cream,
   whipped

For the crust, spread the macadamia nuts in a single layer on a baking sheet and toast at 350 degrees for 2 minutes, stirring occasionally. Remove to a plate and let stand until cool. Maintain the oven temperature.

Process the macadamia nuts in a food processor until ground, reserving the remaining nuts. Combine the ground macadamia nuts, vanilla wafer crumbs, butter and sugar in a bowl and mix well. Press the crumb mixture over the bottom and up the side of a 9-inch pie plate. Bake for 10 minutes or until golden brown. Let stand until cool.

For the filling, sprinkle the gelatin over 2 tablespoons lime juice in a bowl and let stand for 10 minutes. Whisk the condensed milk and egg yolks in a medium saucepan until blended. Add 1/2 cup lime juice and whisk until smooth. Cook over medium heat for 6 minutes, stirring occasionally; do not boil. Stir in the gelatin mixture and lime zest and cook until the gelatin dissolves, stirring frequently. Spoon the lime filling into the prepared pie plate and chill for 6 to 10 hours. Spread the whipped cream over the top, sealing to the edge, and sprinkle with additional macadamia nuts.

Strawberry Festival Pie

Serves 6 to 8

Pecan Crust
3 egg whites
1 cup sugar
1 cup butter cracker crumbs
1 cup chopped pecans
1 teaspoon vanilla extract

Strawberry Filling
1 cup whipping cream
1 teaspoon sugar
1 teaspoon vanilla extract
3 cups sliced fresh strawberries

For the crust, beat the egg whites in a mixing bowl until stiff but not dry. Add the sugar gradually, beating constantly. Fold in the cracker crumbs and pecans and stir in the vanilla. Spread the pecan mixture in a greased 9-inch pie plate and bake at 350 degrees for 30 minutes. Let stand until cool.

For the filling, beat the whipping cream, sugar and vanilla in a mixing bowl until soft peaks form and fold in the strawberries. Spoon the strawberry filling into the prepared pie plate just before serving.

Brown Sugar Brownies

Makes 16 brownies

1 cup flour
2 teaspoons baking powder
1/2 teaspoon salt
1/2 cup (1 stick) plus 2 tablespoons
   butter

2 cups packed brown sugar
2 eggs, lightly beaten
1 teaspoon vanilla extract
1 cup chopped pecans or walnuts

Mix the flour, baking powder and salt together. Microwave the butter in a microwave-safe bowl until melted. Add the brown sugar to the butter and stir until blended. Stir in the eggs and vanilla. Add the flour mixture and mix well. Stir in the nuts.

Pour the batter into a greased and floured 9×9-inch baking pan. Bake at 350 degrees for 30 to 35 minutes or until the edges pull from the sides of the pan. Cool in the pan on a wire rack and cut into squares.

Rocky Road Brownies

Makes 2 to 3 dozen brownies

Brownies
1 cup flour
1/4 cup baking cocoa
1 teaspoon baking powder
2 cups sugar
1 cup (2 sticks) butter or
  margarine, melted
3 eggs, lightly beaten
1 teaspoon vanilla extract
1 1/2 cups chopped nuts
  (optional)

Chocolate Marshmallow Icing
1/2 cup (1 stick) butter or
  margarine
3 tablespoons baking cocoa
1 1/2 tablespoons corn syrup
18 large marshmallows
1 (16-ounce) package
  confectioners' sugar
1 teaspoon vanilla extract
1 1/2 cups chopped nuts

For the brownies, mix the flour, baking cocoa and baking powder. Combine the sugar and butter in a bowl and mix well. Stir in the flour mixture, eggs and vanilla. Add the nuts and mix well. Spread the batter in a 9×13-inch baking pan and bake at 350 degrees for 30 minutes.

For the icing, combine the butter, baking cocoa, corn syrup and marshmallows in a double boiler and cook over low heat until blended, stirring frequently. Remove from the heat and stir in the confectioners' sugar, vanilla and nuts. Pour the icing over the warm brownies and let stand until set. Cut into bars.

Pinellas County has a unique award-winning greenway corridor, the Fred E. Marquis Pinellas Trail. The trail links some of the county's most picturesque parks, scenic coastal areas, and residential neighborhoods. Thirty-five miles of former railroad right-of-way beginning in Tarpon Springs and terminating in St. Petersburg, the trail is easily accessible from parks and major roadways.

Key Lime Shortbread

Makes 1 1/3 dozen

1 cup flour
1/4 cup confectioners' sugar
1/2 cup (1 stick) butter, softened
1/3 cup sugar
2 eggs

3 tablespoons flour
3 tablespoons Key lime juice
grated zest of 1 Key lime
1/2 teaspoon baking powder
confectioners' sugar to taste

Combine 1 cup flour and 1/4 cup confectioners' sugar in a bowl and mix well. Add the butter and mix until combined. Pat over the bottom of an 8×8-inch baking pan and bake at 350 degrees for 15 minutes. Combine the sugar, eggs, 3 tablespoons flour, lime juice, lime zest and baking powder in a mixing bowl and beat until blended. Spread the lime mixture over the hot baked layer and bake for 25 minutes longer. Cool in the pan on a wire rack. Dust with confectioners' sugar to taste.

Holiday Spice Cookies

Makes 4 dozen cookies

3/4 cup dark corn syrup
1 cup sugar
1/2 cup (1 stick) butter
3/4 cup heavy cream
1 teaspoon ground cloves
1 teaspoon cinnamon

1 teaspoon allspice
1 teaspoon ginger powder
1 teaspoon grated orange zest
4 cups flour
1 teaspoon baking soda

Heat the corn syrup in a saucepan. Remove from the heat and mix in the sugar and butter, stirring until the mixture is cool. Chill in the refrigerator until cold, stirring occasionally. Add the cream, cloves, cinnamon, allspice, ginger powder and orange zest and mix well. Stir in a mixture of 4 cups flour and the baking soda; the dough will be thick and hard to mix. Chill, covered, in the refrigerator.

Roll the dough 1/16 inch thick on a lightly floured pastry cloth, adding flour as needed. Cut with the desired cutter and arrange 2 inches apart on a cookie sheet. Bake at 375 degrees for 6 to 8 minutes or until light brown. Cool on the cookie sheet for 2 minutes. Remove to a wire rack to cool completely.

Turtle Cookies

Makes 2 dozen cookies

1 1/4 cups flour
1/4 teaspoon baking soda
1/4 teaspoon salt
1/2 cup (1 stick) butter
1/2 cup sugar
2 ounces semisweet
  chocolate, melted
1 egg yolk

2 teaspoons vanilla extract
3/4 cup finely chopped pecans
16 milk caramels
2 1/2 tablespoons heavy cream
2/3 cup semisweet chocolate
  chips
2 teaspoons shortening

Mix the flour, baking soda and salt together. Beat the butter in a mixing bowl until creamy. Add the sugar, chocolate and egg yolk to the butter and beat until blended. Stir in the vanilla. Add the flour mixture and beat until blended. Chill, covered, for 1 hour.

Shape the dough into 1-inch balls and roll in the pecans. Arrange 2 inches apart on a cookie sheet. Make an indentation in each cookie with the back of a spoon. Bake at 350 degrees for 12 minutes. Cool on the cookie sheet for 2 minutes and remove to a wire rack.

Combine the caramels and cream in a saucepan and cook over low heat until blended, stirring constantly. Spoon the caramel mixture into the indentation in each of the warm cookies and let stand until cool.

Combine the chocolate chips and shortening in a heavy-duty resealable plastic bag. Microwave for 1 to 1 1/2 minutes or until melted and squeeze the bag to blend. Cut 1 of the corners of the bag and drizzle the chocolate mixture over the cooled cookies. Let stand until set. Store in an airtight container.

Visit, view, and learn the biology and behavior of bottlenose dolphins, loggerhead sea turtles, Kemp's Ridley sea turtles, river otters, stingrays, local fish, and coral reefs at the Clearwater Marine Aquarium. The aquarium cares for sick and injured marine mammals.

Sponsors

Black Grouper ($5,000-$15,000)
Publix Super Markets Charities
The Fresh Market
Tampa Bay Magazine

Scamp Grouper ($2,000–$4,999)
The Past Presidents of the Junior League of Clearwater-Dunedin, Inc.,
the Junior League of Clearwater and the Junior Service League of Dunedin

Red Grouper ($1,000–$1,999)
Digital Latitudes, Inc.
MMA Financial, LLC
PurePostcards.com
Ruth Eckerd Hall
Wal-Mart Stores, Inc.

Yellow Edge Grouper ($500–$999)
Edward and Lorre Barrett
Bollenback & Forret, P.A.
Anthony and Georgine Brancato
Clearwater Gas System
Junior League of Clearwater-Dunedin, Inc., Board of Directors (2003-2004)
Junior League of Clearwater-Dunedin, Inc., Cookbook Development Committee
Spencer International Advisors, Inc.

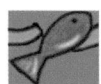

Brown Grouper ($250–$499)

Bonefish Grill of Florida
Clearwater Threshers Baseball
Gary Connors and Amy Jennings
Danka Office Imaging

Kiwanis Club of Springtime City
Lexus of Clearwater and Tampa Bay
Law Offices of Charles F. Robinson
Chris and Christine Ruppel

Snowy Grouper ($100–$249)

Acordia
advertising-images.com, Promotional Products
AutoWay Dodge
Bruce W. Barnes, P.A.
Tim and Angela Breaux
Michelle and Dr. Fred J. Carolan
Century 21 Plumlee Realty
Clearwater Plumbing, Inc.
Cobblestone Court Decorative Hardware
Katie and Clint Cole
Colmer Photography
Joan Crawford, Cornell Hotel Society
Creative Contractors, Inc.
Tom and Pauline Deal
Terri and Daniel Dennehy
Felicia Leonard and Bruce Dennis
Bill and Dianne DeVault
Capt. Greg S. DeVault, Angling Adventures
Dunedin Brewery
Charlie Earhart Realty
Mary Ann Eifert
Alan Everton Insurance, Inc.
First National Bank of Florida
Kathy and Neil Ford
Global Payments, Inc.
Great Bay Distributors, Inc.
Harper, Van Scoik & Company, LLP
Hillcrest Garden Club
Charles R. Hilleboe, P.A.

Amy and Scott Hopkins
Jean Ann Hughes
J.P. Marketing
Law Office of Scott Johni, P.A.
Junior League of Clearwater-Dunedin Inc.,
Membership Development/Provisionals
Dennis C. and Diana Stiffler Larson
Katie and Mark Marshburn
James Millspaugh & Associates, Inc.
Dave and Marty Musial
Rick and Donna Nelson
Palm Harbor Auto Service, Inc.
Dr. and Mrs. Chris Patterson
Dr. and Mrs. J. Wayne Phillips
Pinellas Public Library Cooperative, Inc.
Quality Thin Films, Inc.
Patty Rader
Gary Repetti
Kert D. Rhodes, World Savings
Dawn M. Larson Scott, DM Enterprises
Chris, Debbie and Allison Smith
Paul L. Sokolowski, Aprex, Inc.
Mindy and Michael Solomon
Ward's Seafood Market and Galley
Janet A. Wehmeyer
Deborah White
John and Linda Williams
Linda S. Williams, State Farm Insurance Agency
Winn-Dixie Stores, Inc.

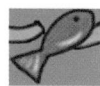

Contributors

The Junior League of Clearwater-Dunedin, Inc., enthusiastically thanks
all our members, families, and friends who contributed recipes,
prepared recipes for testing or retesting, tasted recipes, hosted tasting events
in their homes, and those involved we have inadvertently omitted.

Kathryn Adikes	Nancy Bennett	Mildred R. Burkhart
Heidi Akers	Karen J. Bentley	Margaret Word Burnside
Claudia Allen	Sharon Bergner	Merry June Burwell
Melissa Allen	Sandi Berry	Betty Byrd
Clem Anderson	Cathy Bland	Diane Cagni
Raymond Anderson	Nancy W. Blanton	Susan T. Calhoun
Dory Arroyo	Nancy Bomstein	Lisa Califf
Aileen Bair	Kelly Borota	Michele Cameron
Crystal Banning	Tina Borst	Geri Campos
Terry Banning	Kay Bouth	Debbie Canny
Jennifer Baralt	Claudia Boyd	Traci Carroll
Francis Barreiro	Georgine Palmer Brancato	Amy Casey
Priscilla Barreiro	Tonya White Brancato	Wendy Cassidy
Lorre Barrett	Nelly Brigham	Linda Cipolla
Pam Barrett	Alescia Brown	Michael Cliff
Pat Bauer	Cindy Brown	Nicola Cliff
Janet Baustert	Gemmy Brown	Winifred J. Coachman
Jean W. Beach	Michelle Brown	Aimee Coker
Peggy Bealafeld	Jay Brown	Katie Cole
Ernestine Bean	Kay Brown	Sandy Cole
Ann Beck	Jane Burgos	Debbie Cooney

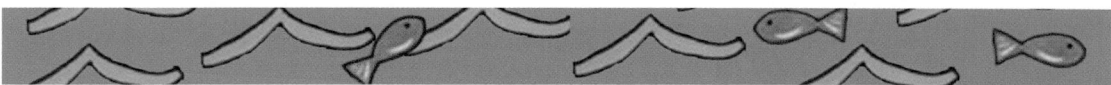

Judy Cottrell
Joan Crawford
Crown Family of Clearwater,
Hazel, Karen, Betty and DeLene
Chris Daily
Bonnie Davis
Stephany Dawson
Zeynep DeBoer
Lisa Deese
Lynne DeFilippo
Taskin Demitras
Bruce Dennis
Sandy Diamond
Allison Dolan
Amy Doussan
Katherine Duff
Wanda DuFrain
Holly Duncan
Carrie Durda
Alexis Elie
Cheri Elliott
Myra Elliott
Sue Ellis
Erin Ester
Laura B. Evans
Sally C. Evans
Beth Falkson

Julie Featherstone
Dotti Fischer
Louise Fischer
Lisa Flittner
Jan Floyd
Heather Foderingham
Thelma Fodiman
Melissa Fontaine
Renee Foran
Kathy Ford
Art Forenza
Kandy Forenza
Cindy Forte
Ginger Francisco
Alison Freeborn
Peggy Freeborn
Sharon Gilberg
Diane Gobo
Anne Goodman
Charlene Gordon
Rhonda Gracie
Carolyn Graisbery
Vivien S. Grant
Debi Gregson
Linda Griggs
Patricia Grohman
Pam Groi

Margie Gubbini
Gwynne Hackworth
Vivian Haicken
Christine Halchak
Jeanette Hale
Molly Hancock
Rosalie Hanley
Mamie S. Harrison
Mary Lynne Hawkins
Myra Hemerick
Janet Henderson
Candice Hennessy
Erin Henson
Theresa Hess
Amie Hessemyer
Teresa Hibbard
Amy Hinrichs
Sarah Hooper
Amy Hopkins
Scott Hopkins
Shannon Horrell
Jerry Hotho
Becky Humphreys
Jane Hunt
Nancy Hunt
Kim Jacke
Amy Jennings

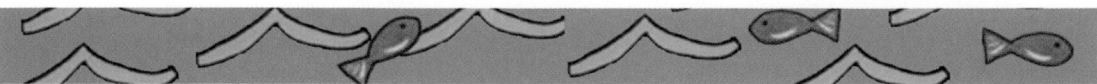

Nola Johnson	Melissa Mannino	Katherine Norcross
Trish Johnston	Martha Margolis	Nicola Nothdurft
Bobbie Kahler	Cory McBride	Carol NuDelman
Deanna Keator	Betty B. McDermott	Kathy Oberndorfer
Gail Keck	Pat McFederick	Pam Ora
Lawrence Keeton	Jennifer McGrail	Laura Oursler
Sonya Kelley	Betty B. Medlent	Cindy Paige
Karen Kelly	Barbara Meyer	Sherry Pantelides
Margaret Kickliter	Doug Meyer	Donna Parker
Leona Kinnear	Jessica Meyer	Nicole Parker
Dave Kmietek	Nora Mihopoulos	Trisha Patterson
Dimitra Kratimenos	Lois Miller	Georgia Paulidia
Deborah Pointer Kynes	Sandra G. Millspaugh	Nancy Pearson
Karen Lampson	Sharon Mladucky	Rene Pearson
Betty Lang	Betty Jean Moore	Carlen Petersen
Peggy Langlykke	Monica Morris	Liz Phillips
Andrea Lapenna	Liz Mulligan	Anne Neil Piccone
Christina Lappas	Connie Murphy	Lisa Platis
Arleen Larson	Allison Murray	Paula Prentiss
Diana Larson	Bill Murray	Suzann Quesada
Gloria Layne	Rosalie Murray	Patty Rader
Hilda Leon	Sue Murray	Laura Redmond
Felicia Leonard	David Musial	Darlene Ress
Trudy Word Little	Lois Musial	Donna Reynolds
Gwin Londrigan	Marty Musial	Teri Reynolds
Susan Londrigan	Deborah Nader	Lisa Rhodes
Jeanette Lynch	Gretchen Neff	Browder Rives

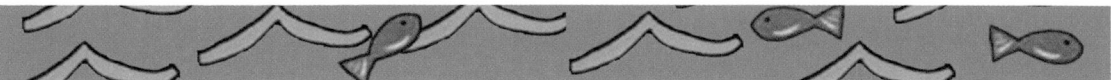

Shelly Roberts
Charles F. Robinson
Louise Robinson
Nicole Robinson
Gail S. Roeper
Ann Marie S. Rogers
Christine Ruppel
Lisa Rygiel
Dina DeFranco Sachs
Howard Sachs
Debbie Salvesen
Karen Sampson
Nancy Sawayda
Katherine Schmidgall
Barb Schuler
Tim Schuler
Dawn M. Larson Scott
Susan Scott
Karen Seel
Barbara Shannahan
Patrick Sheppards
Lynne Shoars
Ryan Shoars
Stacey Shy
Sara Hale Simmons
Libby Singer
Patti Singleton

Diane Sinicrope
Jill Sketch
Margo Skicewicz
Debbie Larson Smith
Stephanie Smith
Deanna Snedeker
Sally Spencer
Jennifer Speranza
Jim Stathopoulas
Susan Stauffer
Terry J. Stiffler
Laura Stigleman
Kathy Strong
Diane Sullivan
Sustainer Gourmet Group—
Potpourri
Nancy Taylor
Annie Galvin Teich
Barbie Tesar
Marcia Timm
Leigh Ann Tomlin
Jan H. Tracy
Effie Trihas
Carol Uhrich
Ellen B. Van Winkle
Diane Vollbracht
Lori Vosen

Teri Vrchoticky
Nancy Waitas
Mary Walsh
Mary Helen Watrous
Marion Watson
Dianne Wheatley-Giliotti
Kristina White
Judy Wiedman
Bea Wilcox
Linda S. Williams
Marilee Williams
Therese Williams
Mary K. Wilson
Peggy Word
Meg Yoklavich
Ken Zand

Contributing Restaurants and Specialty Markets

Alfano's
Linda and Frank Alfano, *Owners*
1702 Clearwater-Largo Road
Clearwater, FL 33756
727-584-2125

Backwater's
Mark Carey, *Chef*
Larry Edger, *Owner*
1261 Gulf Blvd., Suite #130
Clearwater, FL 33767
727-517-7383
www.backwatersonsandkey.com

Black Cat Gourmet, To Go Catering
Bob & Jean Beach, *Owners*
14278 Walsingham Road
Largo, FL 33774
727-595-7677/1-888-757-8197

Bob Heilman's Beachcomber Restaurant
Bobby's Bistro & Wine Bar
Bob & Sherry Heilman, *Owners*
447 Mandalay Ave.
Clearwater, FL 33767
727-442-4144
www.heilmansbeachcomber.com

Belly Timber's Grill
Bob Dickerson & Alfie Crescentini,
Chefs/Owners
29000 US Highway 19, North
Clearwater, FL 33761
727-210-GRILL
www.bellytimbersgrill.com

Bon Appetit
Peter Kreuziger, *Owner*
150 Marina Plaza
Dunedin, FL 34698
727-733-2151

Bonefish Grill
Tim Curci, *Chef & Co-Founder*
Locations: (managing partner listed after
restaurant location)
Safety Harbor—TJ Theilbar—727-726-1315
St. Petersburg—David Harrell—727-521-3434
South Tampa—Tony Harahan—813-876-3535
Carrollwood—Chad Bash—813-969-1619
Belleair Bluffs—David Valentine—727-518-1230
www.bonefishgrill.com

**Casa Tina—Gourmet Mexican & Vegetarian
Cuisine**
Javier and Avila Tina, *Owners*
369 Main Street
Dunedin, FL 34698
727-734-9226

Clearwater Beach Hotel
The Hunter Family, *Owners*
Daniel Fuchs, *Chef*
500 Mandalay Ave.
Clearwater Beach, FL 33767
727-441-2425
www.clearwaterbeachhotel.com

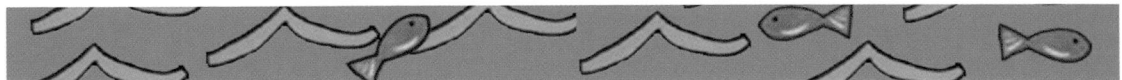

The Columbia Restaurant
The Gonzmart Family, *Owners*
Geriberto Malpico, *Chef*
1241 Gulf Blvd.
Clearwater, FL 33767
727-596-8400
www.columbiarestaurant.com

Frenchy's Restaurants of Clearwater Beach
Michael Preston, *Owner*
419 East Shore Drive
Clearwater, FL 33767
www.frenchysonline.com

The Fresh Market
25961 US Highway 19, North
Clearwater, FL 33763
727-669-6111
www.thefreshmarket.net

Grillmarks
Nick Pappas, *Owner*
Jim Cantrell, *Chef*
607 N. Clearwater-Largo Road
Largo, FL 33770
727-584-6235
www.grillmarks.com

Kally K's Steakery & Fishery
Alex & Nora Mihopoulos, *Owners*
1600 Main Street
Dunedin, FL 34698
727-733-7024

La Maison Gourmet, Inc.
Chef John Lewis, *Owner*
471 Main Street
Dunedin, FL 34698
727-736-3070
www.lamaisongourmet.com

Keegan's Seafood Grille
Linda & Cesar Labrador, *Owners*
1519 Gulf Blvd.
Indian Rocks Beach, FL 33785
727-596-2477

The Lobster Pot
Joan Reiter, *Owner*
Steve Peek, *Chef*
17814 Gulf Blvd.
Redington Shores, FL 33708
727-391-8592

Pappas' Riverside Restaurant
10 West Dadecanese Blvd.
Tarpon Springs, FL 34689
727-937-5101
www.pappasriverside.com

Salt Rock Grill
Frank Chivas, *Owner*
Chef Barry Spaulding, *Chef*
19325 Gulf Blvd.
Indian Shores, FL 33785
727-593-7625
www.saltrockgrill.com

The Westin Innisbrook Resort
Peter Cipolla, *Executive Chef*
36750 US Highway 19, North
Palm Harbor, FL 34684
727-942-2000
www.westin-innisbrook.com

Ward's Seafood Market & Galley
Robert & Michele Cameron, *Owners*
1001 Belleair Rd.
Clearwater, FL 33756
727-581-2640/1-800-556-3761
www.wardsseafood.com

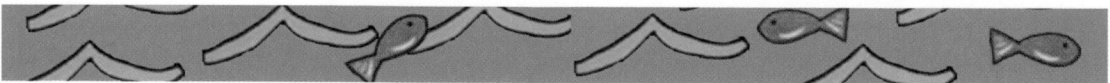

Past Presidents

**Past Presidents of the
Junior League of Clearwater, Inc.**

1948-49: Mrs. Arthur B. Kline	1966-67: Mrs. Richard J. Kamensky
1949-50: Mrs. Wilson H. Valentine	1967-68: Mrs. James W. Cochran
1950-51: Mrs. Kay Thompson	1968-69: Mrs. Cedio Saltarelli
1951-52: Mrs. Maurice M. Condon	1969-71: Mrs. Jean Ann Hall Hughes
1952-53: Mrs. William E. Crown, Jr.	1971-72: Mrs. Penn Dawson
1953-54: Mrs. P.H. Guinand	1972-73: Mary Ann Thornton McArthur
1954-55: Mrs. Everett M. Harrison	1973-74: Dolores Moore Huss
1955-56: Mrs. C. Raymond Lee, Jr.	1974-75: Mary Voight Cummings
1956-57: Mrs. James M. Jackson	1975-76: Jane Smith Lowrey
1957-58: Mrs. Robert J. Clark	1976-77: Merry June Jackson Burwell
1958-59: Mrs. William E. Shurtleff	1977-78: Heather Heuchan Foderingham
1959-60: Miss Julia Gehm	1978-79: Matile Guinand Hendry
1960-61: Mrs. Albert J. Gricius	1979-80: Judith Freeman Sauers
1961-61: Mrs. Donald M. Emerson	1980-81: Mary Alice Wayt Bosselman
1961-62: Mrs. James B. Leonard	1981-82: Amelia Wood Carey
1962-63: Mrs. David E. Edmunds	1982-83: Julie White Featherstone
1963-64: Mrs. Gloria Spiner Burton	1983-84: Karen Cornelius Crown
1964-65: Mrs. Clinton B. Holden	1984-85: Melody Wordsworth Figurski
1965-66: Mrs. Roger O. Bouchard	1985-86: Holly Hecht Duncan

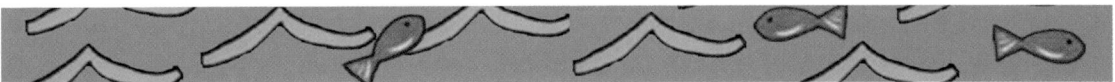

Past Presidents of the
Junior Service League of Dunedin, Inc.

1959:	Mrs. James Norton
1959:	Mrs. Charles Phillips, Jr.
1959:	Mrs. Reinhold Rogers, Jr.
1960:	Mrs. Reinhold Rogers, Jr.
1961:	Mrs. William Dicus
1961:	Mrs. Walton Byars
1962:	Mrs. Kenneth Burton
1963:	Mrs. James Owens
1964:	Mrs. Edwin Groves
1965:	Mrs. Bernard Chilton
1966:	Mrs. Walter Pownall
1967:	Mrs. William Hale
1968:	Mrs. Andrew Myers
1969:	Mrs. J. Floyd Glisson
1970:	Mrs. E. C. Register
1971:	Mrs. Irwin Entel
1972:	Mrs. Coleman T. Brown
1973:	Mrs. Myron Moore
1974:	Mrs. Thomas E. Williams
1975:	Mrs. Robert Deyoung
1976:	Mrs. George Hardin
1977:	Mrs. Nick Dieb
1978:	Mrs. Norwood Cardozo
1979:	Mrs. Dan Jordan
1980:	Mrs. Mark Brandt
1981:	Mrs. Dale Christensen
1982:	Mrs. Stanley Seagren
1983:	Mrs. Charles Guenther
1984:	Mrs. Ed Proefke, Jr.
1985:	Mrs. Jeff Davis

Past Presidents of the
Junior League of Clearwater-Dunedin, Inc.

1986-87:	Marilyn Meisel Lokey
1987-88:	Margaret Jennings Metz
1988-89:	Janice Bonne Case
1989-90:	Deborah Pointer Kynes
1990-91:	Molly Carter Hancock
1991-92:	Nancy Beetham Frock
1991-92:	Jan Haughton Tracy
1992-93:	Karen Williams Seel
1993-94:	Linda Burr
1994-95:	Liz Phillips
1995-96:	Kathy Short-Rabon
1996-97:	Judy Cannaday
1997-98:	Ann Rogers
1998-99:	Whitney Gray
1999-00:	Marion Rich
2000-01:	Susan Benjamin
2001-02:	Nancy Sawayda
2002-03:	Pam Ora
2003-04	Alison K. Freeborn

Bibliography

The American Heritage® Dictionary of the English Language, Fourth Edition
Copyright © 2000 by Houghton Mifflin Company.
Published by Houghton Mifflin Company. All rights reserved.

WordNet® 1.6, Copyright © 1997, Princeton University

Gone with the Grits, by Diane Pfeife, Copyright © 1992,
Strawberry Patch, Atlanta, Ga.

Good Old Grits Cookbook,
by Bill Neal & David Perry, Copyright © 1991,
Workman Publishing Company, New York, NY.

www.foodtv.com
Scripps Networks, Inc., Copyright © 2004. All rights reserved.

Clearwater, A Pictorial History, by Mike Sanders, Copyright © 1983,
The Donning Company, Norfolk,Virginia

Visitors Information Guide and *Relocation Guide*, Copyright © 2004,
Clearwater Regional Chamber of Commerce

www.americanheart.com
American Heart Association, Inc., Copyright © 1998. All rights reserved.

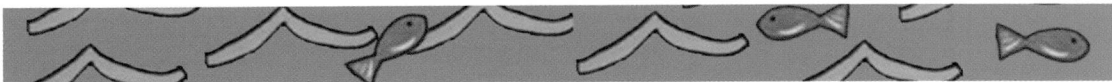

Index

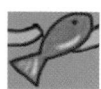

from Grouper to Grits

The Junior League of Clearwater-Dunedin, Inc.
1265 Bayshore Boulevard
Dunedin, Florida 34698
727-738-5523 Fax 727-735-9186
www.jlcd.org jlclwdun@aol.com

Name

Street Address

City   State   Zip

Telephone

Your Order	Quantity	Total
from Grouper to Grits at $24.95 per book		$
Florida residents add 7% sales tax		$
Postage and handling at $5.00 per book		$
Total		$

Method of Payment: [ ] MasterCard   [ ] VISA
                                 [ ] Check payable to The Junior League of Clearwater-Dunedin (JLCD)

Account Number   Expiration Date

Signature

Photocopies accepted.